THE COLOMBO
MAFIA CRIME FAMILY

MAFIA LIBRARY

© Copyright 2023 - All rights reserved.

The content contained within this book may not be reproduced, duplicated or transmitted without direct written permission from the author or the publisher.

Under no circumstances will any blame or legal responsibility be held against the publisher, or author, for any damages, reparation, or monetary loss due to the information contained within this book, either directly or indirectly.

Legal Notice:

This book is copyright protected. It is only for personal use. You cannot amend, distribute, sell, use, quote or paraphrase any part, or the content within this book, without the consent of the author or publisher.

Disclaimer Notice:

Please note the information contained within this document is for educational and entertainment purposes only. All effort has been executed to present accurate, up to date, reliable, complete information. No warranties of any kind are declared or implied. Readers acknowledge that the author is not engaged in the rendering of legal, financial, medical or professional advice. The content within this book has been derived from various sources. Please consult a licensed professional before attempting any techniques outlined in this book.

By reading this document, the reader agrees that under no circumstances is the author responsible for any losses, direct or indirect, that are incurred as a result of the use of the information contained within this document, including, but not limited to, errors, omissions, or inaccuracies

TABLE OF CONTENTS

Introduction 1

Chapter 1 : The Rise of Joe Profaci 9

    Early Life and Criminal Beginnings 10

    The Mafia Commission 12

    Formation of the Profaci Crime Family 13

    Ranks and Powers of the Colombo Family Members 15

    Boss 16

    Underboss 17

    Consigliere 17

    Caporegime (Capo) 18

    Soldato (Soldier) 19

    Associate 19

    Elimination of Rivals 20

    Joseph Masseria 21

    Vincent Mangano 22

    Albert Anastasia 23

    Profaci's Criminal Activities 24

    Expansion and Influence 32

    The Death of Joe Profaci 34

Chapter 2 : Profaci-Gallo War and the Rise of Joe Colombo ... 37

    The Gallo Brothers' Background 38

    Larry Gallo (1910-1968) 39

    Albert Gallo (1912-1990) 40

    Joe Gallo (1929-1972) 40

    The Gallo-Profaci War 41

    Impact on the Family's Structure and Reputation 46

    Joseph Magliocco 47

    The Rise of Joe Colombo 48

    The Dispute With Carlo Gambino 49

    Joe Gallo Returns 51

    Death of Joseph Colombo 53

Chapter 3 : The Era of Carmine Persico 55

    Joseph Yacovelli 56

    Rise to Power of Carmine Persico 57

    Carmine Persico's Criminal Enterprises 59

    Murder of Joseph Cafaro 64

    Murder of Greg Scarpa 64

    Murder of Carmine Tramonti 64

    Carmine Persico's Alliances 65

    The Legacy of Persico's Era 67

Chapter 4 : The Colombo War 69

    Aftermath and Impacts on the Family 72

Chapter 5 : The Law Enforcement Battle 73

Law Enforcement's Pursuit of the Colombo Family 74

High-Profile Arrests and Prosecutions 75

The Most Prominent Criminal Cases the Family Faced With Law Enforcement Authorities 79

Witness Protection Program (WITSEC) 82

Salvatore "Sammy the Bull" Gravano 86

Dino "Big Dino" Calabro 87

Frank "Frankie Blue Eyes" Sparaco 87

Salvatore "Big Sal" Miciotta 88

Thomas McLaughlin 88

John Franzese Jr 89

Chapter 6 : The Colombo Crime Family Today 91

Mafia in Recent Years 91

Decline in the Influence and Power of the Colombo Family ... 93

Current Leadership 99

Michael Franzese 106

Joseph "Joe" Amato 110

Vincent "Vinnie Unions" Ricciardo 111

Dennis "Fat Dennis" DeLucia 112

Salvatore "Sally Bread" Cambria 113

Luca DiMatteo 113

Thomas "Tom Mix" Farese 114

William "Billy" Russo 116

Joel Cacace 116

Salvatore "Sally Boy" Castagno 117

Sebastian and Gabriel Mills (The Twins) 118

Giovanni Cerbone 119

Michael Uvino 120

Chapter 7 : Popular Culture and the Colombo Crime Family 121

Impact of These Portrayals on Public Perception of Colombo Crime Family 124

Conclusion 127

References 129

INTRODUCTION

When we talk about the history of crime and power in the United States, we cannot ignore one of the most important elements that shaped this history: Italian Mafia families. These super-families who achieved international fame in the world of organized crime and built criminal empires are the stuff of any crime novelist's dreams, and, in the world of crime and power, some names always resonate and hold a special place in the world's memory. These families reflect a legacy of organized crime spanning decades, and their stories are filled with audacity and disappointment, success, and failure.

In the underbelly of New York City, a secret society thrived, weaving its criminal tapestry through the fabric of the American Dream. The Colombo Mafia crime family, notorious and enigmatic, held the city captive with a web of power, betrayal, and a relentless pursuit of wealth.

The Colombo crime family, also known as the Profaci crime family, was one of the five Italian-American Mafia families that established themselves in New York City during the early 20th century. Its origins can be traced back to the formation of criminal enterprises within the Italian immigrant communities of New York. While the exact birthdate of the Colombo family is not pinpointed, it became a prominent criminal organization in the mid-20th century.

The Five Families are a collective of five Italian-American Mafia syndicates operating within the United States. These organizations include the Colombo crime family, Bonanno crime family, Gambino crime family, Genovese crime family, and Lucchese crime family. Originating from Sicily, Italy, these families immigrated to the United States during the late 19th and early 20th centuries, swiftly establishing themselves as influential and powerful entities who would play a significant role in American organized crime for well over a century.

The emergence of the Five Families can be traced back to the early 1900s, a period marked by a power struggle among rival Italian-American criminal factions. In 1931, a pivotal meeting was convened by Lucky Luciano, a formidable figure originating from the Castellammarese War. At this gathering, Luciano proposed a structural framework for the Mafia characterized by five distinct families that were each assigned its own territorial jurisdiction and leadership. This proposition was embraced by the other leaders present, ultimately giving rise to the Five Families.

Each of these Five Families is helmed by a boss who is the paramount authority within the family. The boss holds responsibility for making significant decisions and overseeing the distribution of the proceeds from the family's criminal endeavors. Beneath the boss are the underbosses entrusted with supervising day-to-day operations, including the consiglieri, who play an advisory role and are involved in planning each family's activities. Further down the hierarchy are the capos, who manage groups of soldiers. Soldiers, occupying the lowest rung, execute the family's directives.

The activities of the Mafia encompass a broad spectrum of criminal pursuits, including drug trafficking, extortion, loan-sharking, gambling, and construction fraud. These organizations have a lengthy history of involvement in violence and corruption.

One of the most substantial ways in which the Mafia have left their mark on American society is through their engagement in the drug trade. Their participation in heroin trafficking began in the 1950s, and they swiftly ascended to a dominant position within the American heroin market. Additionally, these families played a pivotal role in the cocaine boom during the 1970s and 1980s.

Furthermore, the Mafia has significantly influenced American politics by leveraging their financial resources and clout to corrupt politicians at various levels of the government. This corruption has allowed the families to operate their criminal enterprises with a degree of impunity.

The Colombo crime family began to take shape as one of the factions within the larger Profaci crime family, one of the original Five Families of the New York Mafia. Joseph Profaci was the boss of this family during its early years. Joseph Colombo, an Italian-American mobster, played a significant role in the family's history. He rose through the ranks of the Profaci family and eventually became its boss. The family later took on his name. Under Joseph Colombo's leadership, the family grew in influence and power. It began to involve various criminal activities, including extortion, loan-sharking, and illegal gambling. Despite internal conflicts and law enforcement scrutiny, the Colombo family has continued to be involved in organized crime. Over the years, its members have faced numerous prosecutions and convictions. While not as dominant as some other Mafia families, the Colombo family has maintained a presence in the criminal underworld, particularly in the New York City area. Its members have had connections to other criminal organizations, both domestically and internationally.

It can be said that the Colombo crime family has played a significant role in the history of organized crime in the United States. While it may not be as renowned as some other <afia families, its internal conflicts, public attention, and ongoing criminal activities have made it a notable part of the American organized crime landscape.

When we talk about organized crime, we mean criminal activities that are planned, coordinated, and carried out by groups of individuals or criminal organizations, often with a hierarchical structure and a division of labor. These groups engage in illegal activities for financial gain and power, and they typically operate outside the boundaries of the law. Organized crime can take many forms, and it encompasses a wide range of illegal activities.

Criminal organizations often have a structured hierarchy with leaders, subordinates, and different roles within the group. This hierarchical structure allows for efficient organization and division of labor. The primary goal of organized crime is financial gain. These groups engage in illegal activities such as drug trafficking, extortion, money laundering, and other profitable endeavors.

Organized crime groups tend to have a long-lasting presence. They are not ad-hoc or temporary but establish themselves as ongoing criminal enterprises. They maintain their activities over time, adapting to changing circumstances and law enforcement efforts.

They often engage in a range of illegal activities. Diversification helps spread risk and increase profitability.

Organized crime groups are known for using violence and intimidation to protect their interests, settle disputes, and maintain control over territories or markets. Many Mafia families use legal businesses as fronts for their illegal activities, making it difficult to trace the flow of illicit funds. These organizations may seek to corrupt law enforcement, politicians, and other officials to protect their interests and avoid prosecution.

Our purpose is to provide a comprehensive historical account of the Colombo crime family's origins, development, and significant events throughout its history. This would serve as a valuable historical record for researchers, historians, and those interested in the history of organized crime in the United States.

The manuscript aims to delve deeply into the criminal activities and operations of the Colombo crime family. This includes a detailed examination of their involvement in extortion, loan-sharking, illegal gambling, labor unions, drug trafficking, and other illicit enterprises. Analyzing their criminal operations offers insights into the inner workings of organized crime.

The book will also explore the broader societal impact of the Colombo crime family. This involves discussing their influence within local communities, their interactions with law enforcement and government agencies, and their role in shaping the criminal landscape of New York City and beyond. In addition, it offers in-depth profiles of key individuals within the Colombo family, including bosses, underbosses, capos, soldiers, and enforcers. This approach can provide a deeper understanding of the personalities, backgrounds, and roles of these individuals within the criminal organization.

This book delves into various aspects of the Colombo crime family, with the specific content contingent on the author's focus. Nonetheless, some common themes that might be covered include:

- **Historical Perspective:** An exploration of the Colombo crime family's origins, ascent to power, and internal disputes.
- **Criminal Engagements:** Detailed accounts of the Colombo crime family's participation in various illegal activities, such as drug trafficking, extortion, labor racketeering, gambling, and money laundering.
- **Interactions With Others:** A look at the family's relationships with other organized crime groups and their encounters with law enforcement, shedding light on collaborations, conflicts, and the impact of legal measures.
- **Societal Consequences:** An assessment of the impact the Colombo crime family has had on society, including its contributions to corruption, violence, and economic disparities.
- **Individual Portraits:** In-depth examinations of the lives of individual members of the Colombo crime family, offering insight into their motivations, experiences, and the repercussions of their choices.

In addition to these overarching themes, a comprehensive book on the Colombo crime family would also encompass specific details, such as:

- **Character Profiles**: In-depth biographies of prominent figures within the Colombo crime family, encompassing bosses, capos, and other high-ranking members.

- **Historical Milestones:** An account of pivotal moments in the family's history, including notorious gang conflicts, high-profile assassinations, and government investigations.
- **Operational Insights:** An analysis of the Colombo crime family's organizational structure, decision-making processes, and the mechanics behind its criminal operations.
- **Legal Countermeasures:** A discussion of law enforcement strategies aimed at combating the family's criminal enterprises, as well as the family's responses to these efforts.

CHAPTER 1
THE RISE OF JOE PROFACI

In the annals of American organized crime, few names carry the weight and intrigue of Joe Profaci. Giuseppe Profaci was born in 1897 in Villabate, Sicily. He emerged as a central figure in the ever-evolving landscape of the Italian-American Mafia.

This chapter delves deep into the life and rise of Joe Profaci, a man who would come to be known as one of the most influential and enigmatic figures in the history of the American Mafia. From his humble beginnings as an immigrant to his ascent as a formidable underworld boss, we explore the pivotal moments and key decisions that shaped his journey.

Profaci's rise to prominence was not without its share of challenges. He navigated through the tumultuous times of Prohibition, where the illicit alcohol trade was a source of immense wealth and power for many.

But it wasn't just his criminal endeavors that set Joe Profaci apart; he was known for his astute business acumen and his knack for maintaining a low profile; he maintained his original olive oil business, known as Mamma Mia Importing Company, earning him the nickname "The Olive Oil King." This chapter will delve into his legitimate business ventures and the cunning strategies he employed to shield his criminal activities from law enforcement. We will also uncover the inner workings of Joe Profaci's criminal empire and his ability to wield influence and control over his peers and underlings. His story is one of intrigue, resilience, and a relentless pursuit of power within the secretive world of the Italian-American Mafia.

Early Life and Criminal Beginnings

Joe Profaci immigrated to the United States with his family during his early years. He settled in Brooklyn, New York, which was a hub for Italian immigrants and a hotbed for organized crime activities.

In September 1921, Profaci moved to Chicago and opened a bakery, but his venture failed and did not last long. In 1925, he moved to New York entered the field of importing olive oil, and he obtained American citizenship on September 27, 1927.

Profaci's early years were marked by humble origins. Since his youth, he had been involved in a range of illegal activities, and soon found himself involved with the Italian-American Mafia. Profaci began his Mafia career as a low-level criminal, then gradually climbed the hierarchy of New York's criminal underworld until he reached the top.

Over time, Profaci associated with other mobsters and engaged in more lucrative criminal activities, gradually gaining influence and power. Profaci's criminal career advanced to the point where he could establish his crew or faction within the larger Mafia network. He began to recruit loyal associates and expand his criminal operations.

Although he was the king of the city's olive oil trade, Profaci's ambitions were limitless. Later. Profaci decided to form his faction after gaining sufficient knowledge of the inner workings of the New York Mafia. Profaci attended a meeting at the Statler Hotel in Cleveland, Ohio on December 5, 1928. On the meeting's agenda was a recognition of the Profaci crime family in Brooklyn. Given Profaci's lack of experience in the world of organized crime, it was strange that New York gangs delegated authority to him in Brooklyn, and some attributed this to his Sicilian origins linked to the Italian Mafia.

Profaci's criminal activities evolved to include racketeering, loan-sharking, illegal gambling, and labor union control. These activities allowed him to amass wealth and power within the criminal underworld.

As Profaci's power grew, so did tensions and rivalries with other mobsters and crime families. Conflicts over territory, criminal enterprises, and leadership positions were common in the world of organized crime during this era. These clashes often led to violence, with assassinations, bombings, and other deadly tactics employed to eliminate rivals and maintain control. The Profaci family's rise coincided with a period of intense infighting within the Mafia, as various factions vied for dominance. This turbulent landscape made it even more challenging for Profaci to consolidate his power and prevent his enemies from undermining his authority.

Statler Hotel Meeting

On the evening of December 5, 1928, history bore witness to a secret gathering of some of the most infamous figures in the annals of American crime. It was held in the Statler Hotel in Cleveland, Ohio, and brought together over 40 individuals, several of whom would later ascend to the coveted status of "bosses" within the Mafia.

The choice of venue was not arbitrary; the Hotel Statler stood as a symbol of luxury and grandeur, ranking among the finest establishments in the entire country at the time. While the exact purpose of the meeting remains a subject of historical debate, prevailing theories suggest that these underworld figures had convened to strategize about the partitioning of the immensely lucrative bootlegging trade during the era of Prohibition. With the ban on alcohol production and distribution in full swing, the illicit trade of bootlegged spirits had become a thriving enterprise, prompting the need for organized crime figures to negotiate and solidify their respective territories.

The meeting, however, did not unfold according to plan. In the early hours of that morning, law enforcement authorities descended upon the Statler Hotel, raiding the secret assembly and apprehending twenty-three individuals, including one Joseph Profaci, on charges related to bootlegging activities spanning their respective states.

Profaci wasn't fazed by the arrest. He had successfully achieved his objective of attaining the status of an acknowledged Mafia leader. Later, he was released on bail and went back to New York to expand his empire.

The Mafia Commission

The Mafia Commission is the highest body that manages the affairs of Mafia families in the United States. The structure of this committee has undergone several changes since its founding in

1931, but its main component remains today as the heads of the Five Families.

In 1931, Lucky Luciano decided to create an alternative to the old Mafia system as a central power through which the Five Families could consult to ensure that their interests would not conflict with each other.

The basic idea came from Salvatore Maranzano, one of the most powerful Mafia bosses in New York at the time, specifically after the end of the gang war known as the Castellammarese War. Maranzano's idea was for the major gangs to be divided into crime families. Maranzano was seeking to impose a dictatorial regime under his leadership, and this became clear when he declared himself the leader of all the bosses, which angered the leaders of the Mafia, led by Luciano, who quickly planned to assassinate Maranzano in September 1931 in order to become the new leader of the Mafia.

Luciano was not a dictator like Maranzano, and he saw that the best solution to avoid chaos between families was to give each family the right to manage its affairs on its own while establishing a body that would generally supervise the families and serve as a meeting and consultation center between its leaders. This body was known as the Commission.

Formation of the Profaci Crime Family

The origins of the Profaci crime family can be traced to the formation of a criminal faction within the larger Italian-American criminal scene in New York City. During his youth, Joe Profaci played a pivotal role in organizing this faction.

In the early 1930s, Joe Profaci and his faction became more independent and organized. They have established themselves as a separate and recognized Mafia family. This marked the formal formation of the Profaci crime family.

The Profaci crime family, like other Mafia families, engaged in various criminal activities, including extortion, loan-sharking, illegal gambling, controlling labor unions, and more. They worked primarily in Brooklyn but also had interests in other parts of New York City, as they became responsible for the financing of prostitution and drug trafficking.

As the 1920s drew to a close, New York City's underworld was on the brink of a violent upheaval. In 1930, the Castellammarese War erupted in a ruthless struggle for power between two factions within the Mafia. While the war raged, Joseph Profaci, a shrewd and ambitious mobster, carefully navigated the treacherous landscape, maintaining a neutral stance despite his suspected support for Salvatore Maranzano, the boss of the Castellammarese faction.

Amidst the chaos and bloodshed, Profaci's calculated approach paid off. When the war concluded in 1931, Charles "Lucky" Luciano, the victor of the conflict, reshaped New York's criminal underworld, establishing five distinct organized crime families. Profaci emerged as the recognized head of the Profaci crime family, solidifying his position as a prominent figure in the Mafia's hierarchy.

Profaci's leadership was further strengthened by his strategic alliances with other powerful mobsters. He forged a strong bond with Joseph Bonanno, a partnership that would prove enduring for nearly three decades. Their collaboration extended beyond the boundaries of their respective families, as they worked together to expand their influence and control over various criminal enterprises. Profaci also maintained close ties with Stefano Magaddino, the boss of the Buffalo crime family, further solidifying his position within the Mafia's network.

Under Profaci's leadership, the Profaci crime family flourished, expanding its operations into various lucrative rackets, including gambling, labor unions, and extortion. Profaci's ruthlessness and strategic acumen earned him a reputation as a formidable force in the underworld, and his influence extended far beyond the confines of New York City.

Ranks and Powers of the Colombo Family Members

The intricate hierarchical structure and dynamics of power within the Colombo crime family was deeply intertwined with the fabric of the extended family system, a complex network that hinged on the pivotal factor of familial bonds and kinship ties. Membership within the family was not merely a transactional arrangement; rather, it was profoundly rooted in blood relations, emphasizing the significance of family connections as the primary criterion for inclusion. Within this elaborate system, prospective family members were not only scrutinized for their capabilities but also evaluated within the broader context of their familial lineage. The revered elders of the family, figures endowed with considerable influence, played a central role in the intricate process of member selection, exercising their authority to make decisions that shape the composition and hierarchy of the family. These decisions, guided by the wisdom and experience of the elders, rippled through the familial structure, dictating not only the individual roles and responsibilities of the family members but also determining the rank and powers that each member was entrusted with. In essence, the Colombo crime family operated as a tightly knit unit; its organizational framework was intricately interwoven with the complicated tapestry of familial relationships, where the elders serve as the guiding arbiters of the family's destiny.

The ranks of family members can be divided into three levels: upper ranks, middle ranks, and lower ranks.

Upper Ranks

Boss

The boss occupies the pinnacle of power, wielding immense authority and influence over the organization's operations and the lives of its members. The boss serves as the supreme leader, the embodiment of power and decision-making who is responsible for shaping the family's trajectory and safeguarding its interests.

The boss's authority is multifaceted, encompassing a range of responsibilities that extend beyond mere leadership. They serve as the family's chief strategist, formulating plans to expand operations, secure lucrative deals, and maintain a competitive edge in the ever-evolving world of organized crime. Additionally, the boss plays the role of arbiter, settling disputes between family members and enforcing the organization's internal code of conduct.

The boss's power, however, is not absolute; it is derived from the respect and loyalty of the family members. Maintaining this respect and loyalty requires a delicate balance of strength, charisma, and shrewdness. The boss must be able to command respect through their actions, inspiring fear and admiration among their subordinates. At the same time, he must exude charisma, fostering a sense of camaraderie and loyalty within the family.

Underboss

Within the hierarchical structure of the family, the underboss holds a position of immense significance, serving as the second-in-command to the boss and playing a pivotal role in the organization's operations. The underboss is not merely a subordinate or an assistant; they are a trusted confidante, a strategic advisor, and an integral part of the family's leadership team.

The underboss position is typically attained through years of proven loyalty, unwavering commitment, and a demonstrated capacity for strategic thinking. The underboss must possess a deep understanding of the family's intricate workings, the dynamics of organized crime, and the delicate balance of power that exists within the underworld.

It can be said that the underboss of the family plays a crucial role in the organization's leadership, serving as a trusted advisor, a strategic thinker, and a bridge between the boss and the rank-and-file members. Their contributions are essential for maintaining internal cohesion, navigating external relationships, and ensuring the family's continued success in the world of organized crime.

Consigliere

The consigliere stands as a trusted advisor, a reservoir of wisdom, and a guardian of the family's legal interests. Within the family, the consigliere plays a pivotal role, providing astute counsel to the boss and underboss, and safeguarding the organization's secrets.

The consigliere position is typically bestowed upon an individual who possesses a deep understanding of the law, a keen intellect, and a proven ability to navigate the complexities of the legal system. They must be able to analyze complex legal situations, provide sound advice on potential legal ramifications, and devise strategies to minimize the risk of exposure and prosecution.

In addition to their advisory role, the consigliere plays a crucial part in safeguarding the family's secrets. They are entrusted with sensitive information, acting as a repository of knowledge about the family's operations, its members, and its dealings with the outside world. Their discretion and loyalty are essential for maintaining the family's secrecy and protecting it from infiltration or exposure.

Middle Ranks

Caporegime (Capo)

The capo is a pivotal figure who wields significant authority and influence over a designated group of family members. These individuals, carefully selected through a rigorous process that considers both their capabilities and familial lineage, assume the mantle of leadership and are tasked with overseeing the group's activities and ensuring their seamless integration into the family.

In essence, the capo serves as a bridge between the family's leadership and its members, ensuring that the family's objectives are translated into actionable plans and executed with unwavering commitment.

Soldato (Soldier)

The role of a soldier emerges as an indispensable element, shouldering the responsibility of executing the family's directives and ensuring the seamless implementation of its criminal endeavors. This key position demands a multifaceted skill set, encompassing not only proficiency in criminal enterprises but also an acute awareness of the complex dynamics surrounding the family's operations.

Soldiers also are in charge of the crucial task of collecting intelligence on rival factions, which requires a keen understanding of the ever-shifting landscape within the criminal underworld. Their ability to monitor and assess the activities of competing factions becomes paramount, contributing to the family's strategic advantages and ensuring that it remains ahead of potential opponents.

They are also skilled enforcers. Beyond being implementing the family's will, they serve as the muscle capable of enforcing discipline within the ranks. This includes the capacity to collect debts owed to the family, thus ensuring financial stability.

Lower Ranks

Associate

The associate occupies a unique and often ambiguous position. These individuals, not considered full-fledged members of the family but deeply intertwined with its operations, provide valuable services and expertise, contributing to the family's criminal enterprises while navigating the delicate balance of loyalty and personal gain.

The associate's responsibilities vary depending on their skills and connections, ranging from facilitating illicit transactions to gathering crucial intelligence. They may act as intermediaries between the family and its clients, brokering deals and ensuring the smooth flow of goods and services. They may also serve as enforcers, intimidating rivals and collecting debts, or provide logistical support by managing safe houses and coordinating transportation.

Elimination of Rivals

Joe Profaci's rise to dominance within the American Mafia was a ruthless and bloody affair, marked by a series of violent confrontations with his competitors. Profaci, a shrewd and strategic operator, was not afraid to use violence to achieve his goals. His mastery of deception and manipulation proved invaluable in sowing discord among his adversaries, effectively undermining their positions.

One of Profaci's earliest and most significant rivals was Lucky Luciano, who had held the mantle of the most powerful Mafia boss in the United States until his deportation to Italy in 1946. Profaci seized the opportunity presented by Luciano's absence to expand his influence and solidify his power base. He systematically eliminated Luciano's loyalists and associates, gradually diminishing Luciano's influence even from afar.

Another prominent rival of Profaci's was Vincent Mangano, the head of the Mangano crime family. Mangano's cautious and conservative leadership style contrasted sharply with Profaci's proclivity for violence. This difference in approach made Mangano a prime target for Profaci, ultimately leading to Mangano's assassination in 1951.

With Mangano out of the picture, Profaci assumed control of the Mangano crime family and merged it with his own, creating the Profaci crime family. This expansion of power made Profaci an even more formidable force in the underworld. He turned his attention to other formidable foes, including Albert Anastasia, Carlo Gambino, and Vito Genovese.

Profaci's cunning and ruthlessness were on full display in his orchestration of Anastasia's downfall. He manipulated Anastasia into believing that Gambino and Genovese were conspiring against him. Anastasia, falling for the ruse, confronted Gambino and Genovese, leading to his assassination in 1957.

Profaci's attempts to eliminate Gambino and Genovese proved unsuccessful, as their substantial power and influence thwarted his plans. Nevertheless, his relentless efforts to neutralize his rivals solidified his reputation as one of the most ruthless and feared Mafia bosses in history. Profaci's reign of power was not without its challenges, but his strategic brilliance and ruthless determination allowed him to rise to the pinnacle of the American Mafia.

Profaci's Notable Eliminations of His Rivals

Joseph Masseria

The year 1947 marked a pivotal moment for Joseph Profaci. With a calculated move that would alter the balance of power within the underworld, Profaci orchestrated the assassination of Joseph Masseria, the aging patriarch of the Masseria crime family. This audacious act of violence not only cemented Profaci's position as a formidable force in organized crime but also opened the door for his family to expand its territory and influence.

Masseria, once a revered figure in organized crime, had become increasingly isolated and paranoid in his later years; his leadership style was marked by brutality and a growing distrust of his associates. Profaci, recognizing the opportunity that Masseria's weakness presented, began to carefully lay the groundwork for his demise. On August 6, 1947, as Masseria sat in a restaurant, enjoying a seemingly innocent meal, he was ambushed by four gunmen, their identities concealed beneath fedoras and dark glasses. The gunfire erupted in a sudden burst of violence, shattering the tranquility of the restaurant and leaving Masseria riddled with bullets.

Vincent Mangano

in 1951, Profaci planned the murder of Vincent Mangano, the head of the Mangano crime family. Mangano, who had once been a close ally of Profaci, had grown increasingly independent and ambitious, posing a threat to Profaci's dominance within the world of organized crime. Moreover, Mangano's volatile temperament and impulsive decision-making had become a source of concern for Profaci, who feared that Mangano's actions would draw unwanted attention from law enforcement and jeopardize the stability of their operations.

On April 19, 1951, as Mangano and his brother Philip drove through Brooklyn, they were ambushed by a group of gunmen.

Vincent Mangano was never found, his body disappearing without a trace, while Philip Mangano succumbed to his injuries.

Albert Anastasia

In 1957, Profaci decided to target Albert Anastasia, head of the Anastasia crime family, as a result of a combination of long-standing animosity, and a calculated strategy to assert dominance. Their relationship was strained by a series of disputes over territory and control of lucrative rackets. Profaci, recognizing an opportunity to exploit Anastasia's vulnerabilities, began to carefully lay the groundwork for his downfall.

With a network of loyal informants, Profaci sowed seeds of discord between Anastasia and his rivals, Carlo Gambino and Vito Genovese. He encouraged him to take action against them. He also cultivated alliances with other disgruntled mobsters, forming a web of support to ensure his success in eliminating Anastasia.

In October 1957, Anastasia entered a barber shop in Manhattan, and he was ambushed by a group of gunmen.

Profaci's unrelenting determination to eliminate his competitors played a pivotal role in his rise to power within the American Mafia. His reputation as a ruthless and astute leader, unafraid to employ violence in pursuit of his ambitions, cemented his status as one of the most dreaded and respected Mafia bosses of all time.

Profaci's Criminal Activities

Bootlegging

Joseph Profaci's rise to prominence in the ruthless world of organized crime was inextricably linked to his thriving bootlegging enterprise. During the era of Prohibition, when the manufacture, sale, and transportation of alcoholic beverages were outlawed, Profaci seized the opportunity to establish himself as a major player in the illicit liquor trade. His shrewd business acumen, coupled with his willingness to employ violence and intimidation, propelled him to the forefront of New York City's underworld.

Profaci's foray into bootlegging began in the early 1920s in Brooklyn, where he and his associates established a network of speakeasies and nightclubs that catered to a thirsty clientele. These establishments provided a clandestine yet lucrative outlet for the sale of illegal alcohol, generating substantial profits for Profaci and his partners.

As the demand for illicit liquor soared during the Prohibition years, Profaci's bootlegging operation expanded far beyond the confines of Brooklyn. With a keen eye for opportunity and a ruthless determination to succeed, he ventured into Manhattan, the heart of New York City's nightlife and entertainment scene. To streamline his distribution network, Profaci employed a fleet of trucks that transported liquor throughout the city, ensuring a steady supply to speakeasies, clubs, and private customers.

By the early 1930s, Profaci had established himself as a dominant force in the bootlegging trade, effectively monopolizing the illicit liquor market within Brooklyn. His wealth and influence grew exponentially, as his profits from bootlegging enabled him to acquire legitimate businesses, including restaurants and construction companies. He also ventured into real estate, amassing a substantial portfolio of properties across Brooklyn and Manhattan.

Profaci's success in the bootlegging trade was not without its challenges. Numerous rivals emerged, vying for control of the lucrative liquor market. To maintain his dominance, Profaci resorted to violence and intimidation, eliminating those who threatened his position. He also employed ruthless tactics to collect debts from his customers, ensuring that his profits remained undiminished.

Profaci's bootlegging empire not only enriched him but also provided him with the leverage to corrupt politicians and law enforcement officials. By establishing alliances with influential figures, he further entrenched his dominance in the criminal underworld, ensuring that his illicit activities continued to operate with impunity.

Profaci's reign as a bootlegging kingpin was characterized by ruthlessness, ambition, and a shrewd understanding of the criminal underworld. His legacy is intertwined with the Prohibition era, a time when illicit liquor fueled the rise of powerful underworld figures like Profaci, who left an indelible mark on the history of organized crime.

Racketeering

Profaci's criminal activities in racketeering had a profound and far-reaching impact on New York City. His ruthless pursuit of profit and power extended beyond the realm of bootlegging, infiltrating the city's labor unions, corrupting its political landscape, and ultimately undermining the integrity of its economy.

Profaci's tentacles of influence reached deep into the labor movement, particularly the powerful International Longshoremen's Association (ILA), which represented dockworkers in New York City. With his characteristic ruthlessness, Profaci and his associates orchestrated a systematic takeover of the union, effectively establishing a monopoly on dockworker representation.

This control over the ILA provided Profaci with a potent tool for extortion. Shipping companies, reliant on the services of dockworkers to load and unload their vessels, were essentially held hostage by Profaci's demands for protection money. Failure to comply meant facing disruptions to their operations, significant delays, and increased costs, potentially crippling their competitiveness.

The consequences of Profaci's control over the ILA extended beyond the immediate impact on shipping companies. His influence permeated the union's internal affairs, allowing him to manipulate hiring practices, promote favored individuals to positions of power, and secure favorable treatment for his associates. This corruption eroded the union's ability to effectively represent the interests of its members, instead transforming it into a tool for Profaci's enrichment and consolidation of power.

Profaci's racketeering activities had a detrimental impact on New York City's economy. The extortion of protection money from shipping companies increased the cost of doing business in the city, making it more difficult for legitimate businesses to compete. This stifled economic growth and discouraged investment, hindering the city's potential for prosperity.

Moreover, the corruption that Profaci fostered within the ILA and other labor unions undermined the trust and cooperation necessary for a healthy economy to function. Businesses became increasingly wary of entering into contracts with unions that were suspected of being controlled by organized crime, leading to a decline in unionization and a weakening of the labor movement as a whole.

In essence, Profaci's racketeering activities created a vicious cycle of economic harm. The extortion of protection money increased the cost of doing business, which discouraged investment and hindered growth. This, in turn, made it more difficult for legitimate businesses to compete, further perpetuating the cycle of corruption and economic stagnation.

Gambling

Profaci extended his activities to encompass a thriving gambling operation that served as a significant revenue stream for his organization. He wielded immense control over New York City's underground gambling scene, establishing a network of casinos, sportsbooks, and card games that catered to a diverse clientele of high-rollers, habitual gamblers, and casual players alike.

Profaci's foray into gambling began in the early 1930s when he established secret casinos in Brooklyn. These establishments, operating outside the purview of law enforcement, quickly gained popularity, drawing high-stakes gamblers from across the nation seeking the thrill of illicit wagering. Profaci's astute management and unwavering commitment to secrecy proved instrumental in the success of these early ventures, establishing him as a prominent figure in New York City's underground gambling scene.

Driven by ambition and a relentless pursuit of profit, Profaci expanded his gambling dominion into Manhattan in the late 1930s. His casinos, strategically positioned in prominent locations like Midtown Manhattan and the Garment District, became magnets for gamblers seeking an escape from the drudgery of everyday life. These establishments offered a variety of games, from high-stakes poker rooms to roulette wheels and slot machines, catering to a wide range of preferences and risk appetites.

By the 1940s, Profaci had firmly established himself as one of New York City's most influential figures in the gambling underworld. His casinos generated substantial profits, providing him with the financial resources to further expand his criminal empire and exert greater control over the city's illicit activities.

Profaci's gambling ventures had a profound impact on New York City, shaping its reputation as a hub of vice and corruption. His casinos, operating in the shadows, attracted a criminal element and fostered a culture of illicit activity. The prevalence of gambling in certain neighborhoods, such as Times Square in the 1950s, made it difficult for legitimate businesses to thrive, further contributing to those neighborhoods' decline.

Loan-sharking

Profaci's illicit realm surpassed the boundaries of bootlegging, racketeering, and gambling. It included a profitable and exploitative lending venture aimed at businesses and individuals facing dire financial situations. His unlawful loan shark operations generated a consistent cash flow, empowering his various criminal pursuits and establishing him as a potent figure within the underworld of New York City.

The origins of Profaci's loan-sharking business can be traced back to the early 1930s, when he began providing high-interest loans to businesses and individuals in Brooklyn. His approach to lending was characterized by ruthlessness and disregard for the financial well-being of his borrowers. Profaci often resorted to intimidation and violence to collect outstanding debts, instilling fear and ensuring that his borrowers complied with his demands.

As the 1930s progressed, Profaci's loan-sharking operation expanded beyond its Brooklyn roots, reaching the bustling Garment District and other areas of Manhattan. His network of associates, known as "money collectors," was responsible for disbursing loans and ensuring timely repayments. The high interest rates charged by Profaci often left borrowers trapped in a cycle of debt, unable to escape the clutches of his predatory lending practices.

By the 1940s, Profaci had established himself as one of the leading loan sharks in New York City, amassing substantial wealth and influence from his illicit activities. The revenue generated from his loan-sharking operation provided the primary source of funding for various other enterprises, including smuggling and gambling. His ability to extract exorbitant interest rates from desperate borrowers further solidified his position as a ruthless and powerful figure in the city's underworld.

Profaci's loan-sharking activities had a devastating impact on the lives of his borrowers, many of whom were driven to bankruptcy and ruin. The intimidation and violence employed by Profaci and his associates instilled fear and prevented borrowers from seeking assistance from law enforcement. As a result, Profaci's illicit lending operation flourished unchecked, leaving a trail of financial devastation in its wake.

Construction

The Profaci crime family employed several common methods to derive profits from the construction industry, including extortion, bid rigging, and kickbacks.

Extortion, a prevalent practice, involves coercing money or valuable assets from construction contractors by threatening them with violence or harm. The Profaci crime family frequently engaged in extortion, compelling contractors to provide a portion of their earnings in exchange for protection against potential violence or vandalism.

Another avenue through which Profaci generated revenue in the construction sector was bid rigging. This illicit practice involves the collaboration of two or more companies to fix contract or bid prices, resulting in increased costs for consumers and reduced market competition. The family often manipulated bids for construction contracts, ensuring that their favored contractors secured these contracts.

Kickbacks served as another source of profit within the construction industry. Kickbacks involve the exchange of illegal payments for preferential treatment. The family frequently demanded kickbacks from construction contractors, either as a condition for awarding them contracts or granting approval for their permits. This practice allowed them to secure additional financial gains within the industry.

Money Laundering

The term "money laundering" emerged in the United States during the Prohibition era (1920-1933) when American law enforcement officials began using the phrase to describe the process of concealing the origins of illegally obtained funds. This practice was prevalent among Mafia gangs, who utilized laundromats to obfuscate the true source of their ill-gotten gains from activities like drug trafficking.

Mafia organizations would invest the proceeds of their illicit activities in laundromats, blending their criminal profits with the legitimate income generated by these businesses. This tactic allowed them to "wash" their illegal money, making it appear as if it originated from a legal source. Just as unclean clothes are laundered to make them usable again, the Mafia employed similar techniques to cleanse their illegal funds and make them appear legitimate for further transactions.

To avoid accusations of tax evasion, Profaci maintained his employment at the olive oil company known as Mamma Mia Importing Company. The demand for olive oil surged after World War II, contributing to the growth of his business. Profaci also owned twenty other companies in New York City, expanding his legitimate business interests alongside his illegal activities.

In 1953, Profaci faced legal challenges from the Department of Revenue and the US Department of the Interior, who filed a lawsuit against him for tax evasion, seeking to recover $1.5 million. The following year, the US Department of Justice initiated proceedings to revoke Profaci's citizenship due to false statements he made to immigration officials upon his arrival in the United States in 1921. He had claimed to have no criminal record in Italy.

In 1960, the US Court of Appeals overturned an order for Profaci's deportation. This order had been issued after the seizure of a shipment of oranges imported by Profaci from Sicily. Upon inspection, authorities discovered that the shipment contained 110 pounds of pure heroin. Despite facing these legal challenges, Profaci remained a prominent figure in the underworld, continuing to wield significant influence until he died in 1961.

Expansion and Influence

Profaci's expansion was due to several factors, including:

- **His ruthlessness**: Profaci was not afraid to use violence to intimidate his rivals and protect his interests. This ruthlessness helped him to consolidate his power and expand his territory.
- **His business acumen**: Profaci was a skilled businessman. He was able to infiltrate a wide range of industries, including construction, waste management, and trucking. This gave the Profaci family a steady source of income and allowed it to expand its influence.
- **His connections to other Mafia families**: Profaci was one of the founders of the Mafia Commission, a body that was created to resolve disputes between the different Mafia families. This gave

Profaci a powerful voice in the Mafia and helped him to expand his influence.

Profaci's influence was felt throughout the United States. The Profaci family had a presence in major metropolitan areas, including New York City, Chicago, and Los Angeles. Profaci also had close ties to Mafia families in other countries, such as Italy and Canada. Here are some specific examples of Profaci's expansion and influence:

- The Castellammarese War, which unfolded between 1930 and 1931, pitted Sicilian and non-Sicilian factions against each other in a bid for dominance within the American Mafia. Profaci, displaying strategic acumen and a keen understanding of the shifting tides of power, emerged as one of the leading figures during this tumultuous period. After the war, Profaci emerged as the boss of his own family.
- During the post-war era of the 1940s, through extorting money from businesses, Joseph Profaci, used his formidable position within the Mafia, orchestrated a strategic expansion of the Profaci crime family into a new and lucrative frontier: the construction industry.
- In the 1950s, Profaci infiltrated the waste management industry. He used his control of the industry to launder money and extort money from businesses.
- In the 1960s, the Profaci crime family was one of the most powerful crime syndicates in the United States. The family had a presence in major metropolitan areas throughout the country.

Joe Profaci was a powerful and influential Mafia boss. He expanded the Profaci family into one of the most powerful crime syndicates in the United States. His influence was felt throughout the country and even extended to other countries. Profaci's expansion and influence had several consequences, including:

- An increase in organized crime activity in the United States
- An increase in corruption in the construction and waste management industries
- A decrease in public safety
- A decrease in economic development

Law enforcement agencies have been working to combat organized crime and its negative consequences. However, organized crime remains a serious problem in the United States and around the world.

The Death of Joe Profaci

On June 7, 1962, Joe Profaci, the formidable patriarch of the Profaci crime family, passed away at the age of 64 while serving a five-year prison sentence for racketeering. His death marked the end of an era of significant growth and expansion for his family under his shrewd and ruthless leadership. Under Profaci's reign, the Profaci family had ascended to the pinnacle of organized crime in the United States, establishing itself as one of the most powerful and feared syndicates in the nation.

Profaci's passing coincided with a period of profound transformation for the Mafia. The Federal Bureau of Investigation (FBI) had intensified its efforts to dismantle organized crime networks, and the Mafia faced increasing competition from rival criminal organizations vying for control of illegal activities.

The official cause of Profaci's death was attributed to a heart attack. However, for decades, rumors and speculation have persisted that Profaci was murdered. One theory suggests that he was eliminated by members of his own family, a consequence of his ruthless and demanding leadership style that had alienated many within the organization. Some believe that Profaci's underbosses, seeking to seize control of the family, orchestrated his demise.

Another theory centers on the involvement of rival Mafia families. Profaci's ambition and aggressive tactics had led to clashes with other powerful Mafia bosses, and some speculate that these rivals, fearing his growing influence, conspired to eliminate him to weaken the Profaci family and prevent it from gaining further dominance.

Regardless of the circumstances surrounding Profaci's death, the event undoubtedly sent shockwaves throughout the underworld. It marked the end of an era and ushered in a period of uncertainty and turmoil for the Profaci crime family. With the loss of their charismatic and iron-fisted leader, the family was plunged into a power vacuum, and various factions within the organization engaged in a fierce struggle for control. This period of internal strife and violence continued until Joseph Colombo emerged as the dominant figure, ascending to the top of the family's power structure.

Profaci's legacy is a complex one, marked by both ruthless ambition and a shrewd understanding of the criminal underworld. He was a formidable leader who steered his family to prominence, but his legacy is also tainted by his involvement in racketeering, violence, and the tragic circumstances surrounding his death. His passing marked a turning point in the history of organized crime, signaling the end of an era and the beginning of a new chapter characterized by increased scrutiny from law enforcement and intensifying competition among rival criminal factions.

CHAPTER 2

PROFACI-GALLO WAR AND THE RISE OF JOE COLOMBO

In the sprawling tapestry of the American Mafia's history, there are few stories as captivating and tumultuous as that of the Gallo brothers and their rebellion against the established order. The saga of the Gallo brothers, Larry, Albert, and Joey, reads like a thrilling chapter from a gangster epic, characterized by defiance, ambition, and a willingness to challenge the status quo.

This chapter takes us on a riveting journey into the lives and ambitions of the Gallo brothers, a trio of renegades who dared to challenge the authority of the Italian-American Mafia's old guard. Born and raised in the tough streets of Red Hook, Brooklyn, they would go on to become central figures in a rebellion that shook the very foundations of organized crime.

The Gallo brothers' rise to prominence occurred during a time of transition within the Mafia. The post-World War II era saw the emergence of new criminal powers and a shifting landscape. As we explore the Gallos' ascent, we will uncover the complex web of alliances, rivalries, and personal vendettas that defined this period of upheaval.

One of the most notable aspects of their rebellion was their challenge to the authority of the powerful Profaci family, headed by Joseph Profaci. This rivalry would lead to a series of violent clashes and a power struggle that would captivate the public's attention and leave an indelible mark on Mafia history.

But the Gallo brothers were not mere rebels; they were also known for their audacious criminal exploits and their ability to captivate the media with their larger-than-life personas. Their story is a blend of criminal intrigue, defiance against the Mafia's old codes, and a touch of Hollywood-style drama.

The Gallo Brothers' Background

The Gallo family, a name synonymous with power, intrigue, and a legacy of organized crime, has left an indelible mark on both Italy and America. Their roots can be traced back to the sun-drenched hills of Sicily, Italy, where their criminal influence took shape in the late 19th century. Giuseppe Gallo, a man of shrewd intellect and unwavering ruthlessness, emerged as a formidable figure in the underworld, establishing himself as the patriarch of this infamous clan.

Driven by an insatiable hunger for power and wealth, members of the Gallo family embarked on a path of illicit activities, venturing into the dark realms of robbery, extortion, and protection rackets. Their notoriety grew with each clandestine operation, solidifying their position as a force to be reckoned with in the underworld.

As the 20th century dawned, the Gallo family's influence extended beyond the confines of Sicily, reaching across the Atlantic to the bustling shores of America. Seeking a better life and new opportunities, many family members immigrated to the United States, carrying with them their criminal proclivities and a desire to establish their dominance in the burgeoning underworld of the New World.

In the United States, the Gallo family became known as the "Sicilian Mafia," a name that struck fear into the hearts of many. Their criminal empire expanded rapidly, encompassing a wide range of illegal activities and transforming them into one of the most influential and feared criminal gangs of modern times.

The Gallo brothers were involved in a variety of crimes, including making drug-like Captagon, and weapons trafficking and smuggling. They also practiced extortion, murder, and theft. Their violent style has made them one of the most feared gangs in the world. Over the decades, the Gallo brothers had a significant influence on politics and economics in Italy and America, and they exploited their relationships with politicians and officials to protect their activities. During the fifties and sixties of the last century, the authorities launched campaigns to combat this criminal family and bring its members to justice.

Larry Gallo (1910-1968)

Born in 1910, he emerged as the eldest of the three Gallo brothers, a trio that would carve their infamous names into the annals of the Colombo family.

Gallo's close association with Carmine Persico, a rising star within the Colombo family, further cemented his position within the organization. The two men shared a mutual respect and understanding, their partnership proving instrumental in the family's ascent to power.

As Persico's influence grew, so did Gallo's. He became a trusted confidante, a key advisor, and a formidable enforcer. Under their combined leadership, the Colombo family expanded its territory, its influence infiltrating various industries, from gambling and racketeering to labor rackets and loan-sharking.

In 1968, Larry Gallo succumbed to cancer, his life cut short at the age of 58.

Albert Gallo (1912-1990)

Born in 1912, he occupied the middle spot in the Gallo triumvirate. While his brothers, Larry and Joseph, were renowned for their ruthless ambition and violent tendencies, Albert carved a different path, one characterized by a more calculated and strategic approach. His demeanor was less intimidating, his methods less overt, and yet he commanded respect and wielded considerable influence within the family.

Unlike his brothers, Albert's involvement in violence was less frequent and less direct. He preferred to operate behind the scenes, orchestrating schemes and manipulating situations to his advantage. His calm demeanor and ability to think several steps ahead made him a formidable adversary, one who could beat his rivals with strategic precision.

Joe Gallo (1929-1972)

Also known as "Crazy Joey," Joe Gallo was born on April 7, 1929, in the Red Hook neighborhood of Brooklyn, New York. His early life was marked by a turbulent and criminal upbringing, and he would go on to become a notorious figure in organized crime, known for his involvement in various illegal activities, including extortion, loan-sharking, and violent conflicts within the Mafia. His life was characterized by a series of criminal activities and conflicts, and he was eventually imprisoned for his actions.

Joe Gallo grew up in a tough neighborhood, and he became involved in criminal activities from a young age. As a teenager, he was already involved in petty crimes, and he soon progressed to more serious criminal enterprises. He, along with his brothers, became associated with the Profaci crime family (later known as the Colombo crime family).

The Gallo-Profaci War

The Gallo-Profaci War is one of the most important and violent gang wars in the history of organized crime in the United States of America. This war took place in the 1960s and was between the Gallo family and the Profaci family. The history of this war is filled with violence as well as political and cultural developments that left a significant impact on Italian and American crime communities alike.

After the Profaci family was recognized as a Mafia family, Joe Profaci made an effort to amass wealth through a group of 700 men led by the two brothers Larry Gallo and Joe Gallo. They were among the toughest men who worked with Profaci and played the largest role in robbing shipping containers and banks and carrying out Profaci's tasks. Eventually, Profaci was able to earn an average of fifty thousand dollars a week through his men and began to live a life of wealth at a time while his men, including the Gallo brothers, were almost penniless.

Following the official recognition of the Profaci family as a formidable Mafia organization, Joe Profaci embarked on an ambitious endeavor to amass wealth and consolidate his power. At the heart of his expansionist strategy stood a group of loyal and ruthless enforcers, spearheaded by the formidable Gallo brothers, Larry and Joe. These men, among the toughest and most feared in Profaci's ranks, played a pivotal role in executing his criminal directives, ranging from heists of shipping containers and banks to the elimination of rivals.

Through their relentless pursuit of illicit gains, the Gallo brothers and their cohorts became instrumental in Profaci's financial ascent. Their daring exploits and unwavering loyalty to Profaci enabled him to amass a weekly income of approximately fifty thousand dollars, a staggering sum in that era. While Profaci reveled in the lavish lifestyle his ill-gotten gains afforded him, the Gallo brothers and their fellow enforcers remained largely impoverished, their contributions to Profaci's wealth seemingly undervalued and under-compensated.

The Gallo brothers, particularly Joe Gallo, grew increasingly resentful of the vast wealth Profaci had amassed through their relentless labor, while they remained relatively impoverished. Their discontent festered, fueling a growing sense of injustice and a simmering desire to challenge Profaci's authority.

In a bold move, the Gallo brothers rallied support from a faction of Profaci loyalists, forming a secret group determined to overthrow the reigning boss. Together, they hatched a daring plan to kidnap not only Joe Profaci but also five of his most trusted lieutenants: Frank Profaci, Salvatore Musacchio, Joe Magliocco, Joe Colombo, and John Simon. These men formed the backbone of Profaci's leadership, and their removal would send a powerful message of defiance and challenge Profaci's iron-fisted rule.

On a fateful day in February 1961, the Gallo brothers and their allies set their plan in motion. They meticulously tracked their targets' movements, identifying opportunities to strike. With meticulous precision, they abducted the five men, transporting them to secluded locations, hoping to cripple Profaci's organization and seize control of the family.

However, their audacious plan suffered a significant setback when Joe Profaci, the primary target, managed to elude capture. Despite the meticulous planning and execution of the kidnappings, Profaci's escape proved to be a crucial turning point. The failure to capture Profaci sent shockwaves through the organization, emboldening his supporters and further escalating the internal conflict.

In a phone call, the Gallo brothers asked Profaci for a ransom in exchange for the release of his five men. Profaci's response to Joe Gallo was that he would pay him twice the amount requested if he released his men immediately. Joe Gallo agreed to the deal and released the five men, but Profaci reneged on his promise, and it seemed clear that it was a trick on his part to lure Joe Gallo. Only a few hours after the five men returned to their headquarters, Profaci declared war on the Gallo brothers and everyone who supported them.

On the surface, the deal appeared to be a resolution to the escalating conflict, a chance to restore peace and order within the Profaci family. However, Profaci's motives were far more sinister. His offer of double the ransom was not a gesture of goodwill but a calculated move to lure Joe Gallo into a false sense of security.

Following the release of the five hostages, Profaci promptly reneged on his promise, refusing to pay the agreed-upon ransom. His actions exposed his true intentions, revealing that his offer was merely a ploy to gain time and solidify his own position. This blatant act of betrayal infuriated Joe Gallo and his supporters, further deepening the rift within the family and setting the stage for an all-out war.

Profaci's decision to renege on his promise marked a turning point in the conflict, signaling a decisive shift from negotiation to open hostilities. He declared war on the Gallo brothers and their allies, unleashing a wave of violence that would engulf the Profaci family and send shockwaves through the Mafia.

In a shrewd move to weaken Joe Gallo's support, Profaci managed to sway one of Gallo's closest allies, Carmine Persico, to his side. Persico, a respected and influential figure within the Profaci family, had initially aligned himself with the Gallo brothers in their rebellion against Profaci's leadership. However, Profaci, through his persuasive charm and promises of advancement, convinced Persico to switch sides.

Persico's defection was a significant blow to the Gallo brothers, as it deprived them of a valuable ally and a potential mediator in the conflict. Moreover, it signaled to other members of the family that Profaci was not to be underestimated and that his influence remained strong despite the ongoing power struggle.

With Persico now at his side, Profaci devised a plan to capture the Gallo brothers. He instructed Persico to invite the brothers on a fishing trip, a seemingly innocent gesture that would serve as an opportunity to ambush them. During that trip, on August 20, 1961, Persico held the Gallo brothers at gunpoint. This dastardly act of betrayal shocked and disturbed the Gallo brothers, who considered Persico a close and confidant friend. They immediately nicknamed Persico "The Snake," a nickname that would forever define his reputation for cunning and deceit.

In response to Profaci's duplicity and the betrayal by Persico, the Gallo brothers fortified their bases on 51 President Street, determined to defend themselves and their supporters against Profaci's relentless pursuit. They barricaded the streets surrounding their stronghold, preventing Profaci's men from approaching their headquarters by car. The ensuing conflict between the two factions was characterized by a series of remote explosions and car bombings, transforming the streets of New York City into a battleground of organized crime.

In February 1962, Joe Gallo, driven by a thirst for revenge, attempted to assassinate Joe Profaci's son by planting a bomb in his car. Miraculously, Profaci's son survived the explosion, but the incident further escalated the tensions between the rival factions and intensified the authorities' efforts to bring an end to the violence.

As a result of his involvement in the escalating conflict, Joe Gallo was arrested and sentenced to nine years in prison. His incarceration marked a significant setback for the Gallo brothers' cause, weakening their leadership and leaving them vulnerable to further attacks from Profaci's forces.

After the arrest of their leader, the power of the Gallos declined, and this coincided with Profaci's illness, which led to his death on June 6, 1962, beginning a new era in the family's era, the Joe Colombo era.

Impact on the Family's Structure and Reputation

The Gallo-Profaci war had a significant impact on the Profaci family's structure and reputation.

Impact on Structure

The war weakened the Profaci family and led to a power vacuum. There was competition for leadership, especially after the death of Profaci, and the name Joseph Magliocco emerged as the leader of the family, but he did not rule long, as Joe Colombo took over the leadership later. At the same time, Carmen Persico's star was growing brighter, especially after his pivotal role in the war.

The internal war between the Gallo brothers and Joe Profaci's faction had a devastating impact on the Profaci family, weakening its structure and leaving a power vacuum in its wake. The prolonged conflict drained the family's resources, eroded its reputation, and sowed discord among its members, creating an atmosphere of instability and uncertainty.

Impact on Reputation

The Gallo-Profaci war also damaged the Profaci family's reputation. The violence and bloodshed associated with the war made the family seem more dangerous and unpredictable. This made it more difficult for the family to operate in public and to recruit new members, due to increased scrutiny by law enforcement.

Joseph Magliocco

With Joe Profaci's death in 1962, the Profaci family faced an uncertain future. The mantle of leadership fell to Joseph Magliocco, a seasoned member of the organization who had served as Profaci's underboss. Magliocco, determined to assert his authority and silence any doubts about his capabilities, stepped into the role with a ruthless determination to eliminate the Gallo brothers and consolidate his power.

Magliocco's approach to the conflict with the Gallo brothers was far more brutal and uncompromising than Profaci's. He sought to send a clear message to the other Mafia families that he was not to be underestimated, despite the Mafia Commission's initial reservations about his leadership. His tactics, characterized by violence and intimidation, further fueled the escalating conflict within the Profaci family.

In a parallel power struggle, Joe Bonanno, the patriarch of the Bonanno crime family, devised a daring strategy to eliminate his rivals and establish himself as the undisputed leader of the Mafia. Bonanno's plan centered on the assassination of key figures, including Tommy Lucchese, Carlo Gambino, Stefano Magaddino, and other influential capos within their respective factions.

Seeking an alliance with Magliocco, who harbored resentment towards the Commission for questioning his leadership, Bonanno envisioned a scenario where he would ascend to the top of the Mafia hierarchy with Magliocco as his loyal lieutenant. The two men, bound by a shared desire for power and a willingness to use violence to achieve their goals, embarked on a treacherous path that would shake the foundations of the Mafia.

The initial phase of Bonanno's audacious plan involved the assassination of Lucchese, a task entrusted to Joseph Colombo, a charismatic and ambitious capo within the Profaci family. However, Colombo, driven by his ambitions and thirst for recognition, seized the opportunity to betray Bonanno's plot, revealing it to the Mafia bosses who comprised the Commission.

Fearing for his life, Bonanno fled to Montreal, Canada, leaving Magliocco to face the consequences of their actions alone. Cornered by the Commission, Magliocco eventually confessed to his involvement in the assassination plot.

Given Magliocco's deteriorating health and the limited time he had left, the Commission opted to remove him from the Profaci family's leadership, imposing a hefty fine of $50,000 as a punishment for his actions. Magliocco's downfall marked the end of a turbulent period for the family.

The Rise of Joe Colombo

Appointing a replacement for Profaci was not easy for the Commission. The primary goal of the committee during that period was to bring peace between families in order to keep the authorities' eyes off their activities. Magliocco, Profaci's brother-in-law, plotted with Bonanno to overthrow the Commission, which led to his removal and the appointment of another man, Joe Colombo, as the family's leader. It was Colombo who handed Magliocco over to the

Mafia committee that sided with him, and in his honor, the family name was changed to the Colombo Family.

The good relationship between Colombo and the commission did not last long. Colombo was prone to a life of luxury. He wore thousands of dollars worth of suits and drove luxury cars. Yet he did not have a clear source of income through which he could hide the true source of his wealth as Profaci did through the olive oil trade, which the Commision did not like. Over time, Colombo became known as a criminal, and the FBI put him on trial in 1966 to prove his income. He had nothing to show in court, which led to the opening of an investigation and the interrogation of several Colombo family members, even the arrest of some of them. This prompted Colombo to seriously search for a visible, legal source of income, which he was unable to find, so he began implementing an alternative plan.

He planned to file a lawsuit against the FBI on charges of bias against Italian Americans. This was enough for Colombo to appear as an activist defending the rights of Italian Americans and to gain the support of a large segment of New Yorkers who gathered weekly to support him and protest the FBI. The Colombo case became an issue with a national dimension, and although this was enough to relieve the pressure on Colombo, the Mafia Commission was not happy about it.

The Dispute With Carlo Gambino

Gambino's family leader, Carlo Gambino, was one of the first to advise Colombo to create a front for his business so that he would not fall under police suspicion. Yet Colombo constantly ignored

Gambino's advice, despite the alliance between the two men, as Gambino was considered Colombo's first mentor in the Mafia.

In 1970, Colombo established the Italian-American Civil Rights League, a non-profit organization aimed at protecting the rights of Italian Americans. This organization not only helped him get rid of the FBI, but he now had a legitimate and public source of income as the organization sold Italian and American flags, posters, and T-shirts with slogans defending the rights of Italians.

However, this style of business was unusual for the Mafia, and the Mafia Commission was not satisfied with that. The angriest of them was Carlo Gambino, who was considered his mentor, and who considered that what Colombo was doing was discrediting him because he was the one who taught him everything. Gambino threatened Colombo that he would lose his position if he continued these practices. That point was the beginning of the rift between the two men.

In December 1971, police raided Colombo's headquarters, and records worth $30,000 sent from Gambino to Colombo were found. To prove the legality of these funds, Colombo stated to the jury that these funds were donations from Gambino to the Civil Rights League. This was Colombo's biggest mistake, as he violated one of the most important Mafia rules, which says: "Do not involve your superiors, no matter what happens." This was a shock to Gambino, who considered Colombo's statements an insult to him, as he would never donate to an organization he did not agree to, in addition to the fact that mentioning his name in investigations was something he could not allow.

Joe Gallo Returns

In January of 1971, Joe Gallo was released after serving nine years in prison. Joe Gallo's goal was clear: revenge on the Profaci family, which at that time had become represented by the Colombo family. Colombo was not ready to open a new front, as pressure was surrounding him from all sides, especially from Gambino and the FBI. This prompted Colombo to try to reconcile with Joe Gallo. On the day of his release, he sent him and one of his assistants an envelope containing an amount of money equivalent to $1,000, as a hint that he was ready to support Gallo financially if he backed down from the idea of revenge. However, things did not go as Colombo wished. Gallo tore up the letter in an apparent rejection of Colombo's offer, which was an indication that things were going to get worse.

On August 28, 1971, Colombo was present at Columbus Circle to deliver a speech to thousands of Italian Americans. Nearly 50,000 Italian-Americans attended the event. As Colombo ascended to the podium and began delivering his speech, a man named Jerome Johnson ascended to the podium and directly attacked Colombo and managed to injure him before Colombo's bodyguards intervened and stopped Johnson.

Although Colombo survived the assassination attempt, he was left paralyzed as a result of his serious injury, and he fell into a coma. The New York Police Department opened an investigation into the incident, trying to uncover Jerome Johnson's background and motives, and, although the police never revealed the outcome of the investigation, the finger of blame was pointing to Joe Gallo.

The narrative of Joey Gallo took a tragic turn on April 7, 1972, during what was meant to be a celebration of his forty-third birthday. The venue was Umbertos Clam House, a restaurant where Gallo was enjoying the festivities with his family. However, the revelry was abruptly shattered when four assailants stormed into the restaurant from the kitchen side.

In a desperate bid to escape the impending danger, Gallo tried to elude his attackers, but the swift assailants proved quicker, ultimately claiming his life in a hail of gunfire. This incident, occurring at approximately 4:30 a.m., served as the grim denouement to the saga of the Gallo family, marking the official end of an era.

While suspicions initially pointed towards the involvement of the Colombo crime family in orchestrating this deadly operation, the lack of clear evidence left the true orchestrators shrouded in mystery. Subsequent investigations, however, shed light on a man named Carmine Diabase as a key player in the events leading to Gallo's demise. Collaborating with Sonny Pinto, Patricia's family representative in Manhattan, Diabase emerged as a central figure in the intricate web of motives and alliances.

The motivations behind Carmine Diabase's role in this operation remain elusive, with the complexities of Mafia dynamics adding layers of intrigue to the narrative. It is unclear whether Diabase acted on personal vendettas, business interests, or as part of a larger power play within the organized crime landscape. The intricate dance of allegiances and rivalries within the Mafia often obscured the true motives behind such violent episodes.

Sonny Pinto's involvement adds another layer of complexity to the story. If speculations are to be believed, Pinto may have orchestrated the hit in a bid to provide a service to the Colombo family, potentially aiming to forge stronger ties between the two Mafia families. The intricate alliances and motivations within the Mafia world often defied simple explanations, creating a tapestry of intrigue and danger.

Death of Joseph Colombo

After seven years in a coma, Joseph Colombo was pronounced dead on May 22, 1978.

Joseph Colombo's funeral was held on May 24, 1978, at St. Bernadette's Catholic Church in Bensonhurst, Brooklyn, New York. The church was packed with mourners, including many prominent figures from the Mafia and the Italian-American community.

Colombo was buried in Saint John Cemetery in the Middle Village section of Queens. His funeral procession was over a mile long and was lined with spectators.

Colombo's funeral was a major event in the history of the Mafia. It was a testament to his power and influence, and it was also a sign of the changing times. The Mafia was no longer able to operate as openly and with impunity as it had in the past.

Colombo's legacy is complex. He was a visionary leader who transformed the Colombo family. However, he was also a ruthless criminal who was responsible for countless acts of violence and corruption.

Colombo's rise to power was a product of the Gallo-Profaci War and his abilities. He was a charismatic and ambitious leader, a skilled businessman, and a cunning strategist. This legacy continues to this day, and his family remains one of the most powerful Mafia families in the United States.

CHAPTER 3
THE ERA OF CARMINE PERSICO

After Colombo was shot, Joseph Yacovelli, who had been a member of the Mafia since the 1950s, became the acting boss for one year before Carmine Persico took over. The name Carmine Persico stands out as one of the most enduring and influential in the American Mafia. For decades, Carmine "The Snake" Persico held the reins of power within the family, and his reign was characterized by cunning strategies, internal strife, and a relentless pursuit of control.

This chapter transports us into the era of Carmine Persico, a man who left an indelible mark on the New York City underworld. Born in 1933, he grew up within the family and ascended to leadership during a time of significant change in organized crime. His life was intertwined with both the grandeur and the downfall of the Mafia.

Carmine Persico's tenure as the boss of the family spanned over three decades, making him one of the longest-reigning Mafia leaders in American history. However, his leadership was marked by internal strife, power struggles, and a series of violent conflicts within the family. We will explore the rise and consolidation of his power, as well as the internal dynamics that shaped his leadership.

One of the most intriguing aspects of Carmine Persico's era was his ability to maintain a low profile despite his high position in the Mafia hierarchy. This chapter will delve into his criminal activities, his legitimate businesses, and the complex relationships he maintained with other mob bosses.

Carmine Persico's era was marked by a continual struggle for dominance, both within the family and in the wider context of the American Mafia. His story is one of intrigue, betrayal, and a relentless pursuit of power in a world that often demands unyielding loyalty.

Joseph Yacovelli

Yacovelli was born in Manhattan on January 4, 1928, and grew up with his close friend Jimmy Redd on Mulberry Street, until he became a member of the Mafia. In the early sixties, he moved to New Jersey, where he owned a house. His first criminal record was with the New York City Police in 1945 for theft, forgery, and rioting. Yacovelli initially joined the Josef Ravagi family, becoming a distinguished member by the 1950s. Later, he joined the Colombo family, and his name became famous after the killing of Joe Gallo, as he was among those who contributed to his killing, and he became one of the ten fugitives on the FBI's most wanted list.

Following the Colombo shooting, a gathering convened among the family's top-tier members. During the meeting, underboss Salvatore "Charlie Lemons" Mineo was approached to assume the role of interim boss. However, Mineo declined the offer, citing his advanced age and deteriorating health. Instead, he proposed that consigliere Joseph Yacovelli step in as the acting boss.

Born in Manhattan on January 4, 1928, Joseph "Joey Yack" Yacovelli spent his formative years amidst the vibrant tapestry of Mulberry Street, forging a close friendship with Jimmy Redd. As the allure of the Mafia beckoned, Yacovelli embarked on a path that would intertwine his life with the dark underbelly of organized crime.

In the early 1960s, Yacovelli sought a change of scenery, relocating to the quieter environs of New Jersey, where he established his residence. His first brush with the law came in 1945 when the New York City Police apprehended him for a string of offenses, including theft, forgery, and rioting.

Yacovelli's criminal career began with his association with the Josef Ravagi family, where he swiftly rose to prominence, establishing himself as a respected and influential figure within the organization by the 1950s. His thirst for power and influence led him to seek membership in the Colombo family, a move that would propel him into the spotlight and embroil him in a series of events that would forever alter his destiny.

The infamous assassination of Joe Gallo in 1972 catapulted Yacovelli's name into the public eye. His alleged involvement in the killing, which remains shrouded in controversy, earned him a spot on the FBI's Ten Most Wanted List, transforming him into a fugitive of the law.

Rise to Power of Carmine Persico

Persico was involved in numerous illegal activities. He was known for extortion, robbery, and drug dealing, as well as owning shares in several bars, bakeries, construction companies, and car dealerships, all legitimate businesses that enabled Persico to hide his illicit activities.

Persico and his brother Allie joined street gangs in the early 1950s, like many Italian, Spanish, and Irish youths. They formed small gangs to fight among themselves, and each gang tried to control a specific neighborhood in Brooklyn. Later, a group of gangs merged to form a large gang called the "South Brooklyn Boys." A number of the founders of this gang became prominent names in the Mafia world, including Carmen Persico.

Although he was the youngest, the members of the South Brooklyn Boys all considered Persico their leader, and he was always ahead of them in armed robberies, assaults, and kidnappings. During one of the fights between this gang and another in the city, Persico stabbed a child to death, and his brother Allie ended up being charged with this and sentenced to twenty years in prison.

Thereafter, Persico's power increased, especially when he came under the banner of Joseph Profaci, who gave him broad powers on the streets of Brooklyn, and he became a major player in the Profaci-Gallo War, which broke out in the late 1950s. Persico was the hand with which Profaci struck the Gallo brothers, and was the main reason for setting them up, earning him the nickname "The Snake," due to his duplicity and betrayal of Joey and Larry Gallo, who were his closest friends.

After proving his loyalty to Chief Profaci, Persico rose through the family hierarchy to become one of the youngest and most important leaders in the family. But things did not go the way Persico wanted. In 1971, after a trial that lasted nearly ten years, Persico was sentenced to 15 years in prison after being convicted of several charges, the most important of which were kidnapping, extortion, and graft. Persico was arrested after a raid on his brother-in-law's house where he was hiding and went to prison in 1971. Despite his imprisonment, Persico was able to continue his leadership role through his leadership system and loyal comrades who remained loyal to him even after he entered prison.

Carmine Persico's Criminal Enterprises

During his time as boss, Persico expanded his criminal enterprises to include a wide range of industries, including:

Construction

Persico has been involved in the construction industry across several areas, which have included:

- **Labor Union Control:** Persico asserted his power over many New York City construction unions. This control facilitated his dominance in securing lucrative construction contracts and enabled the family to use blackmail tactics against companies. The impact of this control over the construction unions was far-reaching. It fueled the rise in construction costs, as companies were forced to factor in the additional expenses of extortion payments and union demands. This ultimately had a ripple effect on the economy, affecting the cost of housing, commercial development, and public works projects.
- **Bid Manipulation:** Bid rigging became a standard practice for Persico in construction contracts, ensuring that he consistently won contracts. This strategy provided huge profits and strengthened his grip on the construction sector.

- **Construction Fraud Schemes:** Through his various fraudulent activities in the construction industry, such as inflating costs and using substandard materials, Persico was able to increase his profits from construction operations.
- **Extortion:** This is a method of extortion against companies associated with the construction industry, including demanding bribes on contracts and threatening violence in the event of non-compliance.

Persico's authority over New York City's construction industry extended so deeply that it acquired the nickname "The Concrete Jungle." His construction efforts served as an important source of income that helped fund his broader criminal enterprises.

Waste Management

Persico expanded his involvement in waste management operations by taking control of several waste management companies in New York City and charging the companies exorbitant fees for waste disposal services.

Persico orchestrated schemes to rig bids for waste management contracts, ensuring that he would obtain those contracts. This strategy not only generated significant profits but also expanded his influence within the waste management sector. Furthermore, Persico oversaw numerous fraudulent activities in the waste management industry, which included illegal disposal of hazardous waste at undisclosed locations and falsification of records, further enhancing his gains.

Persico's control over New York City's waste management sector was extensive, and, by the early 1980s, Persico had become the primary controller of waste management contracts, an example of the Mafia's ability to adapt and diversify in response to changing economic conditions.

Drug Trafficking

By establishing extensive contacts with drug traffickers from South America and Europe, Persico expanded the importation and distribution of cocaine and heroin throughout New York City and other areas both inside and outside the United States.

Persico's involvement in the drug trade cemented his status as one of the country's most wealthy and influential criminals. It also had a significant impact on New York City and the United States as a whole, contributing to a widespread drug epidemic and associated violence and criminality with the drug trade. Throughout the 1970s and 1980s, Persico was at the forefront of importers and distributors of cocaine and heroin in New York City and beyond, which gave him the ability to charge high prices for the illicit substances. Furthermore, Persico forced drug traffickers in his areas of influence to offer financial kickbacks and used threats of violence as a means of ensuring compliance.

Gambling

Persico orchestrated a network of control over numerous casinos and illicit sports betting establishments across the nation. This expansive reach allowed Persico to amass substantial wealth by imposing exorbitant fees on gamblers and implementing coercive measures to dissuade potential competitors from encroaching on his lucrative territory.

One of Persico's key tactics involved leveraging his criminal empire's influence to extort legitimate gambling establishments, including racetracks and casinos. Through a menacing combination of threats and violence, he compelled these businesses to pay hefty sums in exchange for protection against criminal activities and the specter of violence.

Loan-Sharking

Remaining steadfast in the tradition of his predecessors, Persico perpetuated a longstanding policy of loan-sharking that extended its influence over both businesses and individuals alike. This approach involved Persico providing loans to enterprises and individuals in need, only to employ coercive and often violent tactics when the recipients of the loan faced difficulties in repayment. In instances where repayment remained elusive, Persico didn't hesitate to escalate his violent tactics.

Hijacking

Persico built an infamous legacy in the hijacking industry throughout his leadership. His foray into this criminal enterprise began during the 1950s when he teamed up with fellow gangsters to rob freight trucks and trains. As time progressed, especially in the 1960s and 1970s, Persico expanded his hijacking endeavors to include aircraft and ships. His network of informants secretly provided him with intelligence regarding potential targets, while an experienced crew of hijackers carried out their missions with minimal violence.

In the 1950s, he and his associates systematically robbed freight trucks and trains in the vicinity of New York City, favoring high-value merchandise such as cigarettes and jewelry. The 1960s also saw an expansion of aircraft hijackings, often targeting flights carrying large sums of cash or valuable cargo. In one notable case, Persico's men hijacked a plane carrying a shipment of gold. In the 1970s, Persico expanded his operations to include ship hijackings, the most famous of which was the hijacking of an oil ship.

This expansion of criminal activities into hijacking exemplifies the Mafia's ability to adapt in response to evolving economic conditions. Taking advantage of the boom in air and sea transportation of goods, the Mafia discovered new sources of revenue. Using violence and intimidation, they effectively dissuaded potential victims from reporting the hijacking to the authorities.

Murder

Carmine Persico's criminal career was marred by a history of deadly acts. He directed and carried out a series of murders, as well as granting permission to other individuals under his command to carry out murders on his behalf.

The use of murder allowed Persico to achieve his goals and enhance his influence within the family. He ordered the killing of rivals, informants, and anyone he considered a threat to his sovereignty. Furthermore, murder was used as a punitive measure against those who defied his orders or did not live up to his expectations.

Persico's murder schemes were complex and deadly, involving a cadre of skilled killers who operated with a remarkable degree of discretion. He also exploited his connections within law enforcement to protect these criminal activities and obstruct the course of justice.

Murder of Joseph Cafaro

Persico orchestrated the execution of Joseph Cafaro, a fellow family member suspected of cooperating with the FBI. Cafaro was ambushed by Persico's enforcers, and a hail of bullets rained down, leaving Cafaro critically wounded. Despite desperate attempts to save him, Cafaro succumbed to his injuries.

Murder of Greg Scarpa

Greg Scarpa, a young and audacious member, had risen to prominence, his rapid ascent casting a shadow over the reigning boss, Carmine Persico. Scarpa's charisma, coupled with his undeniable ruthlessness, had garnered the admiration and loyalty of many within the organization, a notable force that threatened Persico's iron-fisted rule.

In 1963, Persico's insecurities and fears reached a boiling point, and he made the fateful decision to eliminate the perceived threat.

Murder of Carmine Tramonti

In the year 1976, Carmine Persico issued a decree: the elimination of Carmine Tramonti, a fellow family member who had fallen under suspicion of collaborating with the FBI. Tramonti's perceived betrayal had cast a dark shadow over the family, and Persico, determined to preserve the integrity of his organization, deemed it necessary to excise Tramonti. Tramonti was shot to death at a Brooklyn social club. His execution sent a stark message to all within the Colombo family: loyalty was paramount, and betrayal would not be tolerated.

Carmine Persico's Alliances

Carmine Persico's reign as the family's boss was marked by remarkable success, largely attributed to his shrewd ability to forge strategic alliances with other Mafia families and organized crime groups across the globe. These alliances, meticulously crafted and nurtured over time, provided Persico with access to a vast network of resources, expertise, and influence, empowering him to expand his criminal empire and assert his dominance in the underworld.

At the heart of Persico's alliance network lay his partnership with the Gambino crime family, one of the most powerful and influential Mafia organizations in New York City. This alliance, forged through years of mutual respect and shared interests, proved to be a cornerstone of Persico's success. The two families collaborated on a wide range of illicit ventures, including construction projects, waste management schemes, and drug trafficking. These joint operations not only generated substantial profits for both families but also cemented their positions as the dominant forces in the New York underworld.

Persico's alliance with the Gambino family was not his only significant partnership. He also cultivated close ties with the Bonanno crime family, another major player in the New York underworld. The two families engaged in joint criminal enterprises, primarily in the areas of labor racketeering and loan-sharking. This alliance enabled Persico to expand his influence into new territories and broaden his scope of criminal operations. The Bonanno family's expertise in labor racketeering and loan-sharking proved invaluable to Persico as he sought to diversify his criminal portfolio and maximize his illicit gains.

In addition to his alliances within New York, Persico also reached out to organized crime groups in other regions, further expanding his network of influence. He forged a strategic alliance with the DeCavalcante crime family, a New Jersey-based Mafia organization. The two families collaborated in various criminal activities, including labor racketeering and drug trafficking. This alliance solidified Persico's foothold in the tri-state area and provided him with a valuable partner for expanding his illicit activities beyond New York City.

Persico's alliances extended beyond the borders of the United States, as he maintained connections with organized crime groups in other countries, notably Italy and Canada. These international ties opened doors to new markets, resources, and opportunities for collaboration, further enhancing his stature within the global underworld. Persico's connections with Italian Mafia organizations provided him with access to counterfeit goods, drugs, and other illicit commodities, while his links to Canadian crime groups facilitated money laundering and other financial crimes.

The alliances Persico skillfully cultivated granted him immense power and influence within the Mafia. He leveraged his connections to resolve disputes, expand his criminal operations, and strengthen his position against law enforcement. Persico's ability to navigate the complex web of alliances within the Mafia and forge mutually beneficial partnerships proved to be a key factor in his rise to prominence. He became a formidable force in the underworld, a figure respected and feared by his peers and adversaries alike. Persico's strategic alliances transformed the family into a dominant force in the underworld, solidifying his legacy as one of the most successful and influential Mafia bosses in history.

The Legacy of Persico's Era

Persico's reign as head of the family ended in 1985, but his legacy continues to this day. The family remains one of the most powerful Mafia families in the United States. The family still follows Persico's vision of a modern Mafia.

Persico's era as head of the family had a great influence on it:

- **It became more powerful and influential**: Persico's alliances with other Mafia families and his expansion of the family's criminal operations made it one of the most powerful criminal enterprises in the world.
- **It became more organized**: Persico introduced a more structured style and created a more formal structure. He also recruited new members from different ethnic backgrounds.
- **It became more diversified:** Persico expanded his activities into new and more lucrative areas, such as drug trafficking and construction fraud.
- **It became clearer:** Persico worked to change the public image of his business and portray it as a legitimate business organization. He also sponsored charitable events and donated to local organizations.

Despite the legal challenges, Persico remained a formidable opponent of law enforcement. His ability to evade conviction on numerous occasions underscored his skill in overpowering the authorities. Not only was he a skilled criminal, but he was also someone with a deep understanding of the legal system and its weaknesses.

Carmine Persico, while undoubtedly a commanding figure within the intricate web of organized crime, found that the zenith of his success bore with it a weighty price. The turning point came in 1985 when he was convicted and sentenced to 139 years in prison, where he remained until he died in 2019.

CHAPTER 4
THE COLOMBO WAR

The Colombo Civil War, which raged between 1991 and 1993, is a harrowing saga of infighting and ongoing violence within the ranks of the New York Mafia. It happened in the wake of the Carmine Persico era. With Persico behind bars, a power vacuum was created, fueling personal ambitions among internally feuding factions to gain power. The actual beginning of the war was when acting boss Victor Orena challenged the authority of the imprisoned boss of the family, Carmine Persico, giving rise to two rival factions, Orena's supporters and Persico's loyalists.

The conflict was characterized by a string of homicides, bombings, and various acts of violence. In 1992, Orena was found guilty of extortion and handed a life sentence. Nevertheless, the conflict persisted until 1993, at which point Orena's remaining followers were either eliminated or incarcerated. The war concluded with Persico emerging as the victor, but the family suffered significant weakening.

Escalation of Violence

One pivotal moment that catalyzed the escalation of hostilities was the 1991 shooting of Andrew Russo, a high-ranking member of the

Colombo crime family. This act served as the spark that ignited the flames of an open war, setting the stage for a series of violent confrontations that would define the conflict that followed.

The battleground of this internal struggle was marked by a series of attempts on the lives of prominent figures within the crime family. Victor Orena, Jr. and William Cutolo, both influential members, found themselves targeted in assassination attempts that underscored the intensity of the power struggle within the family.

Law Enforcement Intervention and RICO Charges

The Colombo Civil War attracted significant attention and intervention from law enforcement agencies, particularly the FBI and other federal and local law enforcement bodies. The conflict presented a unique opportunity for law enforcement to infiltrate, gather intelligence, and make arrests, resulting in several significant legal actions and repercussions. Law enforcement had been monitoring the family for years, and the internal strife provided them with a wealth of intelligence. Undercover agents, informants, and wiretaps were deployed to gather information on the family's activities and the ongoing conflict.

The FBI strategically infiltrated both factions within the Colombo Civil War. They sought to gain the trust of some members and plant informants who could provide critical information about the factions' inner workings. This allowed them to have eyes and ears on the ground within the organization.

The Racketeer Influenced and Corrupt Organizations (RICO) Act was a powerful legal tool employed by law enforcement. RICO allowed prosecutors to target the entire Colombo Mafia as an organized criminal enterprise rather than focusing solely on individual crimes. This strategy led to the indictment of numerous members, including those associated with both warring factions.

In the end, the conflict led to a wave of indictments and convictions. Numerous members, including high-ranking figures, were arrested and brought to trial on various charges, such as murder, racketeering, and drug trafficking. This legal onslaught weakened the organization's structure and operations.

Members of the Orena faction were arrested and tried as part of law enforcement's efforts to quell the internal strife. Victor Orena, Jr. and several of his associates were among those arrested. The Persico faction also faced a significant number of arrests and convictions. Despite Carmine Persico's incarceration, law enforcement continued to target members loyal to him.

Resolution and Consequences

The Colombo Civil War ended after a truce was reached between the two warring factions. The truce stipulated that power be shared with Victor Orena, Jr. becoming the official boss while Persico maintained his status and influence from prison. The truce was the result of enormous pressure exerted by law enforcement authorities after the outbreak of the conflict, which convinced both parties of the necessity of reaching a solution that would protect everyone from collapse.

But, despite the truce and change of leadership, tensions and mistrust continued. The scars of the conflict were deep, and there was always the risk of renewed hostilities. The division continued, and both sides remained vulnerable to further internal conflict. It was not easy to recover from internal divisions and pressures.

Aftermath and Impacts on the Family

The Colombo War, fought over decades, had profound and lasting effects on the family. The internal conflict, law enforcement intervention, and subsequent truce left a series of consequences and aftershocks that shaped the course of the Mafia in the following years.

The Colombo War has also drawn significant attention in law enforcement. The resulting legal action, arrests, and convictions weakened the organization's infrastructure. Several key members were imprisoned, disrupting criminal operations and revenue streams, and subsequent legal action led to the loss of key personnel. High-ranking members, enforcers, and other vital figures were killed, imprisoned, or forced into hiding. The loss of experienced and trusted individuals had a detrimental impact on the new leadership's ability to effectively manage its criminal enterprises.

Law enforcement agencies continued to monitor the family closely, taking advantage of ongoing tensions and instability. Internal divisions allowed law enforcement officials to gather intelligence and bring cases against members, weakening the organization's reputation and straining its relationship with other Mafia families in New York, for whom it became an unpredictable partner in criminal enterprises.

CHAPTER 5

THE LAW ENFORCEMENT BATTLE

The protracted struggle between law enforcement agencies and the Colombo family has been an enduring endeavor marked by the family's highly organized and disciplined nature. The Mafia's adeptness at evading detection, coupled with its extensive network of contacts and informants, has posed a formidable challenge for law enforcement, creating a persistent and often frustrating barrier to effectively penetrating the organization.

However, recent years have witnessed a noteworthy shift in the dynamics of this ongoing battle, with law enforcement making significant strides in their efforts to dismantle the family. A key catalyst for this change has been the adoption of innovative investigative techniques, such as the implementation of RICO laws and electronic surveillance. These tools have provided law enforcement with a more nuanced and technologically advanced approach, enabling them to navigate the Mafia more effectively.

The landscape of this conflict has been further transformed by the cooperation of former Mafia members who, having severed ties with their criminal past, transitioned into informants. Their insider perspective has proven invaluable, offering law enforcement unprecedented insights into the inner workings of the family's criminal activities. This cooperation has not only bridged critical gaps in intelligence but has also exposed vulnerabilities within the organization that were previously shielded from scrutiny.

This chapter delves into the multifaceted nature of the law enforcement battle against the Colombo Mafia, examining the tactics employed in their pursuit, the challenges they have encountered, and the progress achieved in recent years.

Law Enforcement's Pursuit of the Colombo Family

Law enforcement's pursuit of the Colombo family has been a long and relentless endeavor marked by investigations, surveillance, arrests, prosecutions, and legal tools that disrupt their criminal activities.

Law enforcement agencies used the RICO Act to target the Mafia. RICO allowed prosecutors to charge individuals and entities associated with the Mafia as any criminal enterprise. This strategy aims to dismantle these entities by holding their members accountable for a pattern of criminal behavior.

The FBI and other agencies conducted extensive surveillance and used wiretaps to monitor the activities of Mafia members. This surveillance has provided crucial evidence for investigations and prosecutions, revealing criminal enterprises and hierarchies.

Law enforcement agencies also infiltrated the Mafia using informants and undercover agents. This approach allowed them to obtain inside information about the family's operations, plans, and internal dynamics.

Prosecutors often focused on dismantling leadership. By arresting and convicting high-level members, it weakened members' ability to coordinate and carry out criminal activities.

Prosecutors have pursued specific crimes committed such as extortion, drug trafficking, and murder. Federal, state, and local authorities collaborated to share intelligence, coordinate investigations, and build strong cases against the Mafia. They seized assets linked to Colombo, including real estate, businesses, and financial assets, as a means of disrupting finances.

The chase for the Colombo family by law enforcement agencies is an ongoing battle. The Mafia's resilience and ability to adapt to these pressures, coupled with the tenacity and resourcefulness of law enforcement agencies, make this an enduring and dynamic struggle within the world of organized crime.

High-Profile Arrests and Prosecutions

The Colombo family, like other Mafia families, has seen its fair share of high-profile arrests and prosecutions over the years. Law enforcement agencies have targeted its leadership and key members to dismantle it. Here are some of the high-profile arrests and prosecutions:

Carmine Persico: Carmine "The Snake" Persico, the long-reigning boss, was arrested and convicted on multiple occasions. He was convicted in 1986 on RICO charges and later in 1994 on additional RICO charges. He remained a powerful figure even while serving time in prison.

Alphonse "Allie Boy" Persico: Alphonse T. Persico, also known as "Allie Boy," served as the acting boss of the Colombo crime family from 1996 to 2019 and was the son of crime boss Carmine Persico.

Born in New York on February 8, 1954, he earned the nickname "Allie Boy" to differentiate him from his father's older brother, also named Alphonse, who held the position of caporegime in the Colombo family.

Following Carmine Persico's conviction and life imprisonment, Allie Boy officially assumed the role of acting head of the Colombo family. He continued the family's traditional criminal activities. Notably, he played a part in several high-profile murders, including the 1996 killing of Joseph Scarpa, a prominent family member whose father Gregory Scarpa cooperated with the FBI. Persico ordered Scarpa's death as a message to dissuade others from cooperating with law enforcement.

In 2000, Persico faced charges of racketeering and murder, resulting in conviction on all counts and a 13-year prison sentence. On October 14, 2004, Persico found himself facing charges of orchestrating the murder of William Cutolo, a prominent leader of the family. This assassination was believed to be a manifestation of a vendetta orchestrated by Persico, a vendetta rooted in the turbulent history of the Colombo War during the early 1990s, as Catullo had previously joined the faction led by Victor Urena.

On November 3, 2006, the presiding judge declared a mistrial. The reasons for this shift were the disturbing doubts surrounding the honesty of Margaret Cutolo, wife of William Cutolo, who was accused of lying under oath. However, the case was not over, and a second trial was held, which began on December 28, 2007. This time, the judicial scales were decisively turned, with both Alphonse Persico and his accomplice John "Jackie" DeRoss facing charges of murder, extortion, and witness tampering. On February 27, 2009, Persico was sentenced to life imprisonment.

John "Sonny" Franzese: Born in 1917 in Brooklyn, New York, he was the son of Italian immigrants. Franzese commenced his illegal activities at a young age under the tutelage of his father, a smuggler. In the 1940s, he affiliated himself with the Colombo family, swiftly ascending the ranks to become a caporegime by the 1950s.

During the 1960s, Franzese solidified his influence, establishing close associations with Joe Colombo and cultivating a strong friendship with Colombo's son, Joseph Jr. Despite facing a racketeering conviction in 1985, he secured his release from prison in 1994. However, a resurgence of legal troubles in 1997 led to another arrest, resulting in a 10-year prison sentence. Released in 2007, Franzese lived until 2020, passing away at the age of 103. At the time of his demise, he held the distinction of being the oldest living member of the Colombo crime family.

Victor Orena, Jr.: Victor Orena, Jr., a key figure in the Colombo Civil War, was arrested and charged with multiple crimes, including conspiracy to commit murder. He was convicted and sentenced to prison.

Ralph DeLeo: Ralph DeLeo carved his way through the ranks of organized crime to become a prominent figure in the family. DeLeo's encounter with Alphonse Persico, a powerful figure within the Colombo family, proved to be a pivotal moment in his life. Persico, recognizing DeLeo's potential and unwavering loyalty, welcomed him into the family fold upon his release from prison in

1997. DeLeo's rise within the family was swift and unwavering, and he rapidly reached positions of influence and power.

In the early 2000s, DeLeo's involvement in a series of criminal activities, including racketeering and extortion, caught the attention of law enforcement. He was convicted and sentenced to a lengthy prison term. His scheduled release date is May 28, 2024.

Dino "Big Dino" Calabro: He is accused of being involved in eight murders. Calabro is believed to have played a role in the August 1997 murder of NYPD officer Ralph C. Dols, allegedly following instructions from former Colombo consigliere Joel Cacace. Alongside two other family members, he was apprehended on charges related to drug trafficking, robbery, extortion, murder, and loan-sharking. In November 2017, he received an 11-year prison sentence. Subsequently, he cooperated with law enforcement, emerging as a crucial witness in multiple prosecutions against the Mafia.

Thomas "Tommy Shots" Gioeli: A prominent figure within the family, he became a member in the mid-eighties. Transitioning to the Orena faction in the early nineties, he swiftly shifted his allegiance to Persico's men with the eruption of the Orena-Persico war. Post-war, Persico acknowledged his loyalty by promoting him to the position of caporegime. Arrested on June 4, 2008, he faced multiple charges, including murder and extortion, undergoing several trials before receiving convictions on certain charges. In 2010, Gioli was handed an 18-year and 8-month prison sentence, coupled with a restitution order of $360,000. His expected release date is May 7, 2024.

These high-profile arrests and prosecutions represent the government's ongoing efforts to disrupt Mafia operations and hierarchy. The use of legal tools like the RICO Act has been instrumental in targeting the entire organization as a criminal enterprise, rather than just pursuing individual crimes. Law enforcement agencies have continued to monitor and target the family, using informants, wiretaps, and surveillance to gather evidence and build cases against its members. These actions have weakened the family's structure and influence over time.

The Most Prominent Criminal Cases the Family Faced With Law Enforcement Authorities

Colombo Family Case in 1992:

It is a criminal case in which 14 members of the Colombo family were charged with terrorism, extortion, and murder. This case was one of the largest arrests in the history of organized crime in the United States.

The case began in 1989 when the FBI began investigating the Colombo family's activities in New York and New Jersey. The FBI collected evidence related to the family's criminal activities, including audio recordings and electronic surveillance.

In 1994, a jury convicted 12 of the defendants on all counts. These defendants were sentenced to 15 to 25 years in prison. The remaining defendants, Joseph "Joey" Gallo Jr. and Joseph "Joey" DeFrancesco, were convicted by a federal jury of terrorism and racketeering, but innocent of murder and armed robbery. Gallo was sentenced to 22 years in prison, and DiFrancesco was sentenced to 18 years.

This case was a huge blow to the family. This case led to the arrest and conviction of several prominent members of the family, including Joseph Gallo Jr., who was believed to be the most prominent leader of the family at the time.

Financial Fraud Case of 2000

In 2000, the FBI charged members of the Colombo family with creating DMN Capital Investments Inc. (DMN), which provided investment banking services to small growth companies. The company had no legitimate business purpose and operated solely for "sabotage and money laundering schemes," according to Patrick J. Smith, the assistant U.S. attorney in charge of the investigation.

The investigation, dubbed "Operation Uptick," began in 1999 and involved undercover informants and court-ordered eavesdroppers at DMN's office in Hanover Square, where the FBI recorded more than 1,000 hours of conversations.

Authorities said DMN was run by Robert A. Lino, also known as "Little Robert," a leader in the Bonanno crime family, and Frank A. Persico, a leader in the Colombo family and a registered stockbroker. The three other organized crime families—the Gambinos, Luccheses, and Genovese—were also part of the organization, marking this the first time the Five Families had joined together in a joint securities fraud venture, authorities said.

Persico and the other defendants were arrested without warning on July 21, 2000, and brought directly to court even before hiring lawyers. Persico was allegedly the manager of the brokers who were bribed to sell the shares and control the price. The indictment said that brokers who refused to promote certain stocks on Persico's instructions were threatened, and some suffered violence at the hands of the company's partners. One of the accused allegedly instigated the killing of a person he believed was a cooperating witness in the investigation. Persico admitted to the charges against him and that he was behind defrauding investors worth 50 million euros. He was sentenced to five years in prison, and 11 other family members were also convicted. Persico was released from prison on July 12, 2006; Four months later, Frank died of a heart attack.

Operation Old Fashioned

In 2016, the FBI launched an investigation into the Colombo crime family, which it called "Operation Old Fashioned." The investigation focused on traditional family businesses, such as extortion and fraud. In December 2016, a federal grand jury indicted 20 members of the Colombo family on various charges, including Joseph Amato, Daniel Capaldo, and Thomas Scorcia. The indictment alleged that the defendants had engaged in a wide range of criminal activities, including extortion of businesses in New York and New Jersey, collecting illegal debts through threats and violence, operating a gambling ring, and money laundering.

The defendants' trial began in September 2018. The public prosecution presented evidence from a variety of sources, including secret recordings, phone taps, and surveillance videos. The defendants were sentenced to prison terms ranging from 15 years to life.

Witness Protection Program (WITSEC)

The Witness Protection Program (WITSEC), also recognized as the Witness Security Program, is a federal initiative within the United States designed to relocate and safeguard witnesses facing potential harm due to their cooperation with law enforcement. Administered by the United States Marshals Service (USMS), its authority is derived from 18 U.S.C. § 3521 et seq.

The origins of WITSEC can be traced back to the late 1960s when the USMS began experimenting with safeguarding witnesses collaborating in organized crime cases. In 1970, the Organized Crime Control Act of 1970, passed by Congress, included provisions for the establishment of a formal witness protection program.

Initially modest, with only a few witnesses enrolled in its early years, the program rapidly expanded in size and reach as law enforcement agencies acknowledged its efficacy in protecting witnesses and discouraging criminal activity. By the early 1980s, the program shielded over 3,000 witnesses and their families.

The subsequent decades, specifically the 1980s and 1990s, witnessed ongoing growth in the WITSEC program. It became increasingly involved in safeguarding witnesses involved in cases related to drug trafficking, terrorism, and public corruption. During this period, the program confronted various challenges such as budget limitations, escalating caseloads, and concerns about its effectiveness in preventing witnesses from engaging in criminal activities while under protection.

Despite these challenges, the WITSEC program has retained its significance as a crucial tool for 21st-century law enforcement. The program has continually adapted to meet the evolving needs of law enforcement and protected witnesses. Presently, the WITSEC program safeguards over 19,000 witnesses and their families, earning recognition as one of the most successful witness protection programs globally.

Eligibility for WITSEC

- The witness must have provided testimony in a federal court case against an organized crime member or a drug trafficking organization.
- The witness must face imminent danger from the defendant, their associates, or other individuals or groups.
- The witness must display a willingness to fully cooperate with the USMS and adhere to all program requirements.
- The operational aspects of the WITSEC program involve several key steps: Once a witness is deemed eligible for WITSEC, the USMS devises a new identity for them and their family, encompassing a fresh name, Social Security number, driver's license, and other identifying details. The USMS subsequently facilitates the relocation of the witness and their family to a different city or state. Following their relocation, the witness and their family receive financial support, job training, and various additional support services. The USMS maintains ongoing security monitoring and protection as needed.

The duration of a witness's participation in WITSEC varies according to individual circumstances. While some may require protection for only a few months, others may need it for an indefinite period.

However, participating in WITSEC also presents certain challenges, such as the emotional challenge of their former identities and adapting to a new life. Also, the disruption and difficulties associated with relocating to a new city or state, particularly for children. We should also mention the potential financial hardships while adjusting to new identities and circumstances, in addition to the feelings of isolation from friends and family, which result in a difficult and lonely experience.

Despite these challenges, WITSEC remains a vital program that has safeguarded countless witnesses and their families. It has played a pivotal role in the prosecution of criminals and the pursuit of justice.

Notable Examples of Individuals Protected by WITSEC

- Sammy "The Bull" Gravano: A high-ranking member of the Gambino Mafia who testified against John Gotti, leading to his conviction for racketeering and murder.
- Henry Hill: An associate of the Lucchese crime family who testified against other associates, aiding in racketeering and murder convictions, which inspired the film "Goodfellas."
- Frank Lucas: A drug kingpin who cooperated with authorities, assisting in the conviction of drug traffickers, and disrupting the heroin trade in the United States.

WITSEC has made a significant contribution to the battle against organized crime and drug trafficking, safeguarding numerous witnesses and enabling the prosecution and conviction of some of the world's most dangerous criminals.

Role of Turncoats

Turncoats, also known as informants or cooperating witnesses, provide invaluable insider information about the Colombo crime family. This information can include details about family structure, hierarchy, leadership, criminal activities, and specific crimes.

Becoming a turncoat comes with significant risks. Individuals who cooperate with law enforcement and testify against organized crime families face potential retaliation, putting their lives and the lives of their families in danger. This is where the Witness Protection Program comes into play, providing safety and security.

Turncoats have played a pivotal role in securing convictions against members of the Colombo crime family and other organized crime groups. Their testimony can be a linchpin in building a strong case and dismantling criminal organizations.

The cooperation of turncoats and their involvement in the Witness Protection Program are essential tools in the government's ongoing efforts to combat organized crime. By providing a safe and secure environment for individuals who decide to come forward and testify, the program ensures that witnesses can contribute to criminal prosecutions without fearing retribution from the criminal organizations they once associated with, ultimately weakening these criminal enterprises.

Turncoats Against the Colombo Family

Numerous individuals have cooperated with law enforcement and turned against criminal organizations over the years. These turncoats, driven by fear, remorse, or a desire for justice, provided valuable information and testimonies that helped in prosecuting and disrupting the criminal activities of the Colombo family. Their willingness to break the code of silence and expose the inner workings of the organization proved instrumental in bringing down powerful figures and dismantling criminal networks. Some notable turncoats include:

Salvatore "Sammy the Bull" Gravano

Emerging from the gritty streets of Bensonhurst, Brooklyn, Salvatore "Sammy the Bull" Gravano carved a path of notoriety as an underboss of the Gambino crime family. Born on March 12, 1945, his rise within the Gambino family was swift. However, he decided to become a government informant. Disillusioned with the leadership of John Gotti, the Gambino family's boss, Gravano made the momentous decision to turn against his former associates. In 1992, he agreed to testify as a government witness, providing crucial evidence against Gotti and other mobsters in exchange for a lighter sentence on his murder charges. The weight of Gravano's testimony was undeniable. Gotti, once a seemingly untouchable figure, was convicted of racketeering and murder, then sentenced to life in prison. Gravano's betrayal, while controversial, delivered a significant blow to the Gambino family, dismantling a powerful criminal organization from within. The impact of Gravano's testimony extended beyond the Gambino family, reaching into the ranks of the Colombo crime family. His cooperation with authorities led to the conviction of several Colombo family members.

Dino "Big Dino" Calabro

Born in 1967, Calabro's life was intertwined with the dark side of organized crime, a world in which loyalty, power, and betrayal played a delicate dance. In his youth, he joined the family and became one of its most prominent members.

Finding himself at the heart of Colombo's civil war in the 1990s, Calabro joined the faction led by Carmine "Junior" Persico, carrying out assassinations, organizing kidnappings, and participating in armed confrontations with rival factions.

However, Calabro chose to cooperate with law enforcement; he became a government informant and agreed to testify against his former associates. His detailed accounts of murders, extortion schemes, and other criminal activities led to the convictions of several high-ranking Colombo family members. In exchange for his cooperation, Calabro entered the witness protection program, leaving behind his old life and assuming a new identity.

Frank "Frankie Blue Eyes" Sparaco

Sparaco became an integral part of the family, but his life took an unexpected turn when he chose to cooperate with law enforcement, becoming a government informant and providing crucial testimony that led to the conviction of Colombo members.

In 1992, he agreed to testify as a government witness, providing detailed accounts of his involvement in numerous murders and the inner workings of the family. His cooperation with authorities led to the conviction of 12 Colombo family members, including underboss Alphonse "Allie Boy" Persico.

Salvatore "Big Sal" Miciotta

Miciotta emerged as a figure of both notoriety and influence. However, his story took an unexpected turn when he stood at a consequential crossroads, opting to navigate a path of cooperation with law enforcement.

Miciotta's transformation from an insider to a government witness marked a seismic shift among the Mafia. He became a key player in undercover investigations, a shadowy operative between law enforcement and the Mafia. The recordings captured by Miciotta became major evidence, playing a pivotal role in disrupting several Mafia operations.

Thomas McLaughlin

From his formative years, McLaughlin's persona solidified into that of a formidable and strong young man, cultivating a reputation that seamlessly aligned with the ethos of his familial association. This predisposition facilitated his seamless integration into the family. The early 1990s bore witness to the eruption of the Persico Orena War, a conflict that would serve as the crucible for McLaughlin's emergence as a pivotal figure. Amidst the tumult of war, he assumed a significant role, becoming an active participant in the bloodshed that defined the conflict. Notably, McLaughlin, a member of Gregory Scarpa's notorious crew known as The Grim Reaper, found himself embroiled in the commission of two murders, thereby etching his name into the annals of organized crime lore.

The year 1996 marked a turning point in McLaughlin's criminal trajectory, as he found himself ensnared in a drug smuggling operation. Caught red-handed, he was subsequently sentenced to a twelve-year incarceration. Emerging from the confines of prison in 2008, McLaughlin was confronted with the harsh realities that awaited him within the familial domain. The landscape had shifted significantly during his absence, unveiling a startling abundance of dissidents who had chosen to collaborate with law enforcement authorities. The palpable disillusionment that enveloped McLaughlin became a catalyst for a profound change in his allegiance.

This newfound discontent compelled him to reassess his loyalties and, driven by the fear of a return to prison, McLaughlin made a fateful decision to cooperate with law enforcement authorities. The year 2009 marked the commencement of a clandestine operation, wherein McLaughlin started wearing a wire to record the conversations of numerous family members. This provided law enforcement authorities with a body of evidence that contributed to stopping many of the family's operations and arresting many of its members.

John Franzese Jr

John Franzese Jr., now known as Mat Pazzarelli, was born into the Colombo crime family which many of his relatives joined.

As a young man, he was drawn into the family's illegal activities. His path was planned by the legacy of his father, John "Sonny" Franzese, the remarkable figure in the family.

But the escalating violence and the constant threat of legal repercussions led him to make the courageous decision to sever ties with his family's criminal enterprise, and he became the first son of a prominent New York mobster to testify against his own father. His testimony proved to be a critical blow to the family, exposing their illicit activities and leading to the convictions of numerous high-ranking members.

CHAPTER 6
THE COLOMBO CRIME FAMILY TODAY

Mafia in Recent Years

The Mafia has been a longstanding force in organized crime for centuries. Nevertheless, recent years have witnessed a marked decrease in its influence and authority. Several factors have contributed to this decline:

- Law enforcement agencies have become notably more proficient in their efforts to combat the Mafia, owing to advancements in technology and investigative methods as well as enhanced collaboration between law enforcement entities on a global scale.
- Government legislation, such as RICO in the United States, has made it tougher for the Mafia to operate by allowing law enforcement to prosecute its members for involvement in a criminal organization even in the absence of direct links to specific crimes.
- Changing societal attitudes have shifted the public perception of the Mafia from a once-glorified entity depicted in movies and television to a criminal organization preying on society. This transformation has hindered the Mafia's recruitment efforts and tarnished its public image.

The Mafia's membership has dwindled, partly due to the factors mentioned above, along with the aging of its members. Older Mafia members are retiring or passing away, and their ranks are not being replenished by younger members at the same rate.

The Mafia's control over key industries like construction, gambling, and waste management has dwindled, partly due to law enforcement efforts and competition from other criminal organizations.

Internal disputes, including leadership and territorial conflicts, have plagued the Mafia, weakening its cohesion and making it more susceptible to law enforcement.

Increased public scrutiny from media coverage and investigative journalism has made it harder for the Mafia to operate discreetly.

The Mafia's historical influence on politics has waned, partially due to law enforcement actions and heightened public awareness of its criminal activities.

The Mafia's decline has yielded several positive outcomes for society, including enhanced safety in communities and a more conducive environment for businesses without the looming threat of extortion. However, it has also brought about some negative consequences. The decline has created a void filled by other criminal organizations, such as drug cartels and street gangs. Additionally, it has complicated law enforcement's efforts to monitor and track organized crime activities.

In the United States, the number of Mafia members has dwindled from over 100,000 in the 1980s to approximately 20,000 today. In Italy, the Mafia's control over pivotal industries, like construction and waste management, has significantly decreased. In Japan, yakuza groups have witnessed a similar membership decline of over 50% since the 1990s.

The Mafia's decline underscores the effectiveness of law enforcement actions and the evolving societal norms that have hindered its operations. However, it remains crucial to maintain vigilance, as the Mafia still poses a threat to society.

Decline in the Influence and Power of the Colombo Family

The Colombo crime family, like many other Italian-American Mafia families, has experienced a significant decline in influence and power over the years. Several factors have contributed to this decline:

- Law enforcement agencies have been actively targeting organized crime families, including the Colombo family. High-profile prosecutions and convictions have resulted in the imprisonment of many of the family's members and leaders. This has disrupted their criminal operations and weakened their structure.
- The Colombo family has been particularly notorious for internal disputes and infighting. These conflicts have led to violence within the family and have diverted their attention away from their criminal enterprises.
- The nature of organized crime has evolved over the years. Traditional Mafia activities, such as extortion and loan-sharking, have become less profitable due to advances in law enforcement and changes in society. The rise of other criminal

enterprises, like drug cartels and cybercrime, has also diverted attention and resources away from traditional Mafia operations. Racketeering laws and asset forfeiture measures also have been used to target the financial resources of organized crime families. This has made it more difficult for them to conduct their operations and maintain their wealth.

In recent years, more individuals with knowledge of organized crime activities have cooperated with law enforcement as witnesses or informants. This has enabled authorities to build stronger cases against the Colombo family and other Mafia groups.

As Italian-American communities have assimilated into mainstream American society, the traditional social structures that supported organized crime have weakened. Economic opportunities and legal employment have become more attractive alternatives for young Italian-Americans.

The constant pressure from law enforcement and internal disputes have led to frequent leadership changes within the Colombo family. This instability has hindered their ability to plan and execute criminal activities effectively. Organized crime groups, including the Colombo family, have had to adapt to increased law enforcement scrutiny. They have become more cautious about their communication methods and operations, employing counter-surveillance techniques and using encryption technology.

Leadership Changes and Adaptations

The family has undergone a period of significant transformation in recent years, marked by a series of leadership changes and internal adjustments. These shifts have been driven by a complex interplay of factors, including the relentless pressure from law enforcement and the need to adapt to a rapidly evolving criminal landscape.

In 2019, the passing of Carmine Persico, the family's aging patriarch, marked a turning point in the organization's history. Persico, who had been imprisoned since 1986, had long been unable to exert active control over the family's affairs, leaving a void in leadership that fueled a fierce struggle for power among rival factions.

Emerging from this internal turmoil was Andrew Russo, a relatively young and ambitious figure who quickly rose through the ranks to claim the mantle of leadership. Unlike his predecessors, Russo had joined the Colombo family in the late 1990s, a relatively recent entry into the world of organized crime. Despite his relative newcomer status, Russo exhibited a keen understanding of the changing dynamics of the underworld and the need for adaptation in the face of mounting law enforcement scrutiny.

Under Russo's stewardship, the Colombo family embarked on a series of modifications aimed at navigating the increasingly complex and challenging terrain of organized crime. These changes included the adoption of more sophisticated communication methods, the utilization of advanced encryption technology, and a renewed emphasis on counter-surveillance techniques. These measures, while intended to shield the family's activities from prying eyes, also reflected a growing awareness of the need for caution and prudence in the face of relentless law enforcement efforts.

Russo's leadership also coincided with a period of heightened internal stability within the Colombo family, a stark contrast to the tumultuous years that preceded his rise to power. This relative calm allowed the family to focus its energies on adapting its operations to the evolving landscape of organized crime, a task that proved crucial for its survival and continued relevance in the underworld.

One of the most significant changes implemented by Russo was a decisive shift away from traditional criminal activities such as gambling and blackmail. Recognizing the heightened scrutiny and legal risks associated with these pursuits, Russo steered the family towards more white-collar crimes, including fraud and money laundering. This strategic move reflected an astute understanding of the changing dynamics of the underworld and the need to exploit emerging opportunities.

Internally, Russo implemented a series of structural reforms aimed at enhancing organizational efficiency and resilience. He created new positions within the family's hierarchy, delegating greater authority to his subordinates. This decentralization of power not only streamlined decision-making but also made it more difficult for law enforcement to penetrate the organization's core structure.

In response to the increasing sophistication of law enforcement tactics, Russo directed the adoption of advanced encryption methods for communication and the development of innovative money laundering techniques. These measures, while intended to shield the family's activities from prying eyes, also underscored Russo's commitment to modernization and his willingness to adapt to the evolving technological landscape of crime.

Despite the family's efforts to adapt and remain viable in the face of mounting challenges, it has not been immune to the relentless pursuit of law enforcement. In 2003, Carmine Persico Jr., a prominent figure within the family, was convicted of racketeering and sentenced to life in prison. This conviction, along with other high-profile arrests and prosecutions, served as stark reminders of the enduring threat posed by law enforcement.

Despite these setbacks, the Colombo family, under Russo's leadership, has demonstrated a remarkable ability to adapt and persist in the face of adversity. Its embrace of new criminal activities, structural reforms, and technological advancements has enabled it to maintain its position in the ever-changing world of organized crime.

In 2009, Alphonse Persico, a capo and later an acting boss of the family, was convicted of murder and sentenced to life imprisonment. His conviction came after he was accused of killing one of his colleagues in a territorial dispute. In 2011, Joseph Russo, another leader, was convicted of extortion and sentenced to 20 years in prison. His conviction included supervising multiple criminal activities, including drug trafficking and extortion.

In 2015, Joseph Corozzo, a prominent member, was convicted of extortion and sentenced to 15 years in prison. The charges against him relate to involvement in a drug smuggling operation and laundering the proceeds of the drug trade.

In 2021, Vincent Ricardo, a leader in the organization, faced indictment on racketeering, extortion, and money laundering charges, in addition to being accused of extorting money from a high-ranking official within a Queens-based labor union.

Challenges

The family has faced a multitude of challenges, adapting and persisting through shifting dynamics and heightened scrutiny. One of the most pressing issues facing the family is its aging leadership. Many high-ranking members have been incarcerated or are nearing retirement age, creating a void of experience and expertise that poses a significant threat to the family's continued dominance. This aging leadership has made it increasingly difficult for the organization to attract and retain younger members, a crucial element for ensuring its long-term viability.

Compounding this challenge is the relentless pressure exerted by law enforcement agencies, particularly the FBI. In recent years, the Colombo family has been the target of numerous investigations and arrests, disrupting their operations and diminishing their influence. The enhanced focus on organized crime has led to increased surveillance and infiltration, making it more challenging for the family to conduct their illicit activities without detection.

The changing criminal landscape has also presented a formidable obstacle for the Colombo family. The advent of technology has revolutionized communication and information exchange, providing law enforcement with powerful tools to track and monitor criminal activities. Moreover, the demographic shifts in New York City have altered the traditional power dynamics within the underworld, forcing the family to adapt to a more diverse and competitive environment.

Despite these formidable challenges, the Colombo family has demonstrated remarkable resilience, drawing upon its long history, strong traditions, and deep-rooted connections within the criminal underworld. The family's ability to adapt and evolve in the face of adversity has been a key factor in its enduring presence in the world of organized crime.

To effectively address these challenges, the Colombo family must prioritize the recruitment and development of younger members, ensuring the continuity of leadership and the infusion of fresh ideas and perspectives. Additionally, the family must adapt its operations to the evolving technological landscape, adopting new methods of communication and encryption to evade law enforcement surveillance. Furthermore, the family must carefully navigate the changing demographics of New York City, forging alliances with other criminal organizations to maintain its influence in the underworld.

The Colombo family's future trajectory hinges on its ability to effectively address these challenges and adapt to the ever-changing criminal landscape. While the aging leadership, increased law enforcement scrutiny, and evolving criminal dynamics pose significant obstacles, the family's long history, strong traditions, and deep-rooted connections provide a foundation for resilience and continued influence in the world of organized crime.

Current Leadership

Following the passing of Andrew Russo in 2022, a shroud of uncertainty descended upon the Colombo crime family, leaving the question of leadership hanging in the air. Several names emerged as potential successors, each vying for control of the organization.

Unveiling the New Leader of the Family

Among the contenders, Theodore "Skinny Teddy" Persico, the nephew of the legendary Carmine Persico, stood out as the most prominent figure. His familial ties to the Colombo dynasty and his reputation as a shrewd and ruthless operator made him a formidable candidate for the coveted position.

The federal authorities, keenly aware of Persico's influence and potential to assert dominance, quickly identified him as the de facto leader of the Colombo family. However, this assessment was challenged by an alternative narrative that suggested the family had abandoned the traditional single-boss structure and instead opted for a covert leadership council composed of several influential figures.

Proponents of this theory argued that the Colombo family, scarred by the internal conflicts and power struggles of the past, sought to avoid the pitfalls of centralized leadership and instead distribute power among a trusted group of individuals. This approach, they claimed, would foster greater stability and reduce the likelihood of internal conflict.

In July 2023, contrary to previous speculations, American journalist Jerry Capeci, renowned for his expertise in the realm of organized crime, dispelled misconceptions in July 2023. According to Capeci, the family is currently under the management of Robert Donofrio, also known as "Little Rob," a former capo affiliated with both the Persico and Orena factions.

Robert Donofrio, a Brooklyn native born in 1956, became a pivotal figure within the Colombo family after his recruitment in 1988. His influence became particularly pronounced during the Persico-Orena conflict, where he sided with Persico against Orena. Despite facing legal troubles that led to his arrest and an eight-year prison sentence for conspiracy to murder in 1993, Donofrio's trajectory within the family continued. He was released in 2000, maintained supervised release until 2003, and currently assumes the role of the acting boss of the Colombo crime family.

The Top Advisors

The family's second-in-command, Benjamin Castellazzo, serves as the underboss. Born in Manhattan in 1938, Castellazzo joined the family in the early 1960s. His significance within the family grew, and, during the 1970s, he played a vital role as the coordinator of its activities in New York. Castellazzo was a staunch supporter of Carmine Persico during the conflict with Orena in the early nineties. However, his involvement in a 2021 arrest for conspiring to seize control of a New York City labor union and engaging in racketeering led to a 13-year prison sentence.

Another prominent figure within the Colombo crime family is Ralph DiMatteo, known as "Big Ralphie," who currently serves as the consigliere. Born in Brooklyn in 1960, DiMatteo joined the family during the 1980s and rapidly ascended to the rank of capo in the early 1990s. His allegiance shifted between Orena and Persico during the internal conflict known as the Orena-Persico War, which led to his arrest and a 10-year prison sentence for conspiracy to murder in 1993. Released in 2003, DiMatteo regained his position within the family, eventually earning the trust of Carmine Persico and securing the role of counselor, the family's third-highest rank.

Other Notable Members

John "Sonny" Franzese:

A key figure in the American Mafia, John Franzese held a significant role as a longstanding member and former underboss of the Colombo family. Born on February 6, 1917, in Naples, Italy, Franzese's journey into organized crime began under the mentorship of Joseph Profaci in the late 1930s.

His early criminal record includes a 1938 arrest for assault. Drafted into the United States Army in 1942 during World War II, Franzese was discharged later that year, with a classification of "psychoneurotic with pronounced homicidal tendencies."

In 1947, court papers accused Franzese of rape against a waitress, but no arrest followed in connection to the crime. Over the years, he ascended within the Colombo family, earning the position of caporegime in the mid-1950s under Profaci's guidance. By 1963, Joseph Colombo had promoted him to the coveted position of underboss.

During the 1950s and 1960s, Franzese maintained a facade of legitimacy by listing his official occupation as the owner of a dry-cleaning store in Brooklyn. However, his criminal enterprises expanded in 1967 when he gained a financial stake in the newly established recording company, Buddah Records, using it as a front to launder his illegal earnings.

Accusations of murder swirled around John "Sonny" Franzese when he was implicated in the killing of Ernest Rupolo, a hitman-turned-informant for the Genovese crime family in 1964, allegedly acting on the orders of Vito Genovese. The gruesome details of Rupolo's demise involved being shot and stabbed multiple times, his feet tethered to two concrete blocks, and his hands bound before being dumped into Jamaica Bay.

Franzese, along with nine others, found himself arrested on April 13, 1966 in connection with this heinous crime. Throughout the ensuing trial, the prosecution presented records suggesting Franzese's involvement in the deaths of anywhere between 30 to 50 individuals. Despite the weight of the accusations, Franzese ultimately secured an acquittal for the murder charge.

Yet on March 3, 1967, John "Sonny" Franzese faced conviction in Albany, New York, for orchestrating a series of four bank robberies across the United States in 1965. Subsequently, Judge Jacob Mishler handed down a formidable sentence of 50 years at the United States Penitentiary in Leavenworth in 1970, following numerous unsuccessful appeals. According to his son, Michael, it was during this imprisonment that Franzese defiantly declared, "You watch. I'm gonna do the whole 50."

During Franzese's imprisonment, his nephew, Salvatore Franzese, reportedly assumed control of Franzese's gambling operations. The year 1978 saw Franzese granted parole, only to re-enter prison in 1982 due to a parole violation. Despite this setback, he experienced another release on parole in 1984. Until 2008, Franzese managed to avoid facing additional criminal charges, although his freedom was interrupted by repeated returns to prison on account of parole violations, occurring at least six times during this period.

In 2006, Franzese was accused of Mafia-related murders with Gaetano "Guy" Fatato, an associate in the Colombo crime family. Unbeknownst to Franzese, Fatato was cooperating with the government and secretly recording their conversation. During their exchange, Franzese openly admitted, "I killed a lot of guys—you're not talking about four, five, six, ten."

Following the 2004 incarceration of John "Jackie" DeRoss, Franzese experienced a resurgence in his criminal standing. In 2005, Thomas Gioeli promoted him to the position of Colombo family underboss, marking his return to such a prominent role for the first time since his imprisonment in 1967. However, this upward trajectory was short-lived, as Franzese soon found himself back behind bars in May 2007 due to a parole violation.

By June 2008, while still incarcerated, Franzese faced a new set of legal challenges. He was indicted on charges related to his alleged participation in murders during the Colombo Wars of the early 1990s, involvement in fur coat thefts in mid-1990s New York City. He was also charged with impersonating police and breaking into homes in Los Angeles in 2006.

On June 4, 2008, Franzese, along with fellow Colombo mobsters, was formally indicted on charges encompassing racketeering, conspiracy, robbery, extortion, narcotics trafficking, and loan-sharking. However, by December 24, 2008, Franzese was released from the Metropolitan Detention Center in Brooklyn. Law enforcement sources asserted that, despite his legal complexities, Franzese retained the official title of underboss within the Colombo family.

John Franzese Jr., the son of Franzese, took a dramatic turn by becoming a government informant. In 2005, he cooperated with law enforcement, wearing a wire during interactions with his father. Franzese Jr. went on to testify against his father not once, but twice, facing the alarming threat of his father attempting to have him killed. In the aftermath, he sought refuge under witness protection.

In a startling revelation in 2010, Franzese Jr. disclosed that he had received $50,000 from the FBI as a cooperating witness. This marked a historic moment, as he became the first son of a New York mobster to turn state's evidence and testify against his own father.

Leveraging Franzese Jr.'s testimony, a legal saga unfolded for the elderly Franzese Sr. On January 14, 2011, at the age of 93, he was sentenced to eight years in prison for charges involving the extortion of two Manhattan strip clubs, loan shark operations, and extorting of a restaurant on Long Island. Prosecutors sought a more stringent sentence of 12 years, while Franzese's defense appealed for leniency, citing various health issues such as partial blindness, deafness, gout, and heart and kidney problems.

Despite pleas for compassionate release in July 2016, Franzese was denied, and he remained incarcerated. Ultimately, he saw freedom again on June 23, 2017, when he was released from the Federal Medical Center in Devens, Massachusetts, at the remarkable age of 100. At the time of his release, he held the distinction of being the oldest federal inmate in the United States and the sole centenarian in federal custody.

On February 24, 2020, Franzese passed away in a New York City hospital at the age of 103. A solemn farewell unfolded as he was laid to rest on February 28 at St. John Cemetery, with a funeral service held at the Church of Our Lady of Mount Carmel. His legacy endures through the eight children, 18 grandchildren, and six great-grandchildren he leaves behind.

Michael Franzese

Born on May 27, 1951, Michael Franzese emerged as a prominent figure in the American underworld, having served as a caporegime within the Colombo family. As the son of the former underboss Sonny Franzese, his life took a turn when—having originally enrolled in a pre-med program at Hofstra University—he abandoned his academic pursuits to support his family financially. This decision was prompted by his father's 1967 conviction, which sentenced him to 50 years in prison for a bank robbery.

Forming connections within his father's social circle, including individuals like Joseph Colombo, Michael Franzese asserts that he was formally initiated into the fold on Halloween night in 1975 under the leadership of acting boss Tommy DiBella. Taking the solemn blood oath alongside his comrades Jimmy Angelino, Joseph Peraino Jr., Salvatore Miciotta, Vito Guzzo Sr., and John Minerva, Franzese cemented his ties within the secret world he had entered. In the year 1980, Franzese ascended to the role of caporegime, leading a formidable crew comprising 300 members.

In 1981, Lawrence Salvatore Iorizzo approached Franzese with an elaborate plan to exploit a gap in gasoline tax regulations set to take effect in 1985. Iorizzo, facing threats from California criminals, sought Franzese's assistance in resolving the issue and offered him a share of the proceeds. Collaborating, they established 18 stock-bearer companies headquartered in Panama, where prevailing laws allowed tax-free transactions of gasoline between wholesale entities. Franzese joined forces with the Russian Mafia in Brooklyn to execute this gas scheme.

The modus operandi involved selling wholesale gasoline to one company but redirecting the shipment to another, while a third, acting as a dummy corporation, would fictitiously sell the gasoline on paper and forge tax documents for the receiving company. Franzese's crew managed to pocket a lucrative nine cents per gallon of gasoline in federal tax. To elude enforcement agents, the dummy company would declare bankruptcy, perpetuating the deceptive cycle. This gasoline operation supplied a significant portion, between one-third and one-half, of all gasoline circulating in the New York metropolitan area.

According to authorities, Franzese retained a 75% of the profits, raking in $1.26 million monthly, while Iorizzo secured $45,000 per month. Testimonies later revealed that Franzese personally amassed a staggering $1 million weekly from the lucrative gas scheme.

At the zenith of his career, Franzese boasted of raking in a staggering $8 million per week. Government revenue experts approximated that a whopping $250 million in gasoline tax was pilfered annually in the state of New York. This illegal enterprise then expanded its operations to Florida, where estimates ranged from $40 million to $250 million in stolen gasoline tax losses. Investigating authorities suspected that the ill-gotten gains were laundered through Franzese's film production entity, Miami Gold, eventually finding their way into offshore bank accounts situated in Austria and Panama.

In December of 1985, legal troubles surrounded Franzese as charges were filed against him in both Florida and New York, stemming from allegations of counterfeiting and extortion related to the gasoline bootlegging enterprise. In New York, Franzese found himself among 9 individuals indicted on 14 counts, while in Florida, a more extensive legal action unfolded. He was one of 26 individuals indicted on 177 counts after a 16-month investigation known as "Operation Tiger Tail."

Meanwhile, Lawrence Salvatore Iorizzo, who had already been sentenced to five years and a $1.7 million restitution order for his involvement in the theft of $1.1 million in gas taxes, had entered the witness protection program. In March 1985, Iorizzo began providing testimony against Franzese and others involved in their operation.

On March 21, 1986, Franzese chose to plead guilty to one count of racketeering conspiracy and one count of tax conspiracy. The federal charges resulted in a 10-year prison sentence and a restitution order of $14.7 million, necessitating the liquidation of assets such as his mansion in Old Brookville, New York, and the Miami Gold production company. Additionally, he received a nine-year sentence for state racketeering charges in Florida, to be served concurrently with the federal conviction. A further $3 million in restitution was mandated for the state of Florida. Franzese's period of incarceration concluded in 1989 when he was released on parole after serving 43 months behind bars.

On the 27th of December in 1991, he faced another legal setback when he was handed a four-year federal prison sentence in New York. This sentence stemmed from his violation of probation requirements imposed following his release in 1989. The circumstances leading to this sentence unfolded with Franzese's arrest in Los Angeles on charges of tax fraud. Subsequently, he was transported back to New York to undergo a probation hearing.

During the court proceedings, prosecutors expressed their dissatisfaction, highlighting Franzese's belated initiation of court-ordered restitution payments earlier that year. The delay in meeting these financial obligations raised concerns about Franzese's commitment to fulfilling the conditions of his release. In their arguments, prosecutors contended that Franzese, due to these parole violations, was no longer regarded as a federal cooperating witness by the government. This marked a significant shift in his legal status, as his previous cooperation seemed to be undermined by the issues surrounding his probation and financial responsibilities. The sentencing on that December day in 1991 marked another chapter in Franzese's tumultuous legal journey, adding a layer of complexity to his already intricate legal history.

After his release on November 7, 1994, John Franzese opted for a major life transition, officially retiring from the Mafia in 1995. This decision was coupled with a geographical move to California, where he relocated with his wife and children. The choice to uproot his life was not solely motivated by a desire for a fresh start; it was also prompted by the unsettling reality of receiving multiple death threats.

Since regaining his freedom in 1994, Franzese has undergone a profound transformation, publicly disavowing and condemning the organized crime lifestyle that once defined him. Embracing a new purpose, he has emerged as a motivational speaker, engaging with audiences that span the spectrum from youth in schools to inmates in prisons. His compelling story and insights have found resonance in various venues, where he passionately shares the lessons learned from his tumultuous past.

Notably, Franzese has extended his speaking engagements to Christian conferences and churches, including the well-known Willow Creek Community Church, where he has been a featured speaker since 2016.

The year 2019 marked a significant entrepreneurial venture for Michael Franzese as he took on the role of co-founder for a burgeoning national franchise of pizza restaurants named "Slices Pizza." The franchise initially took root in California and rapidly expanded, boasting a network of five branches across the country at its pinnacle. Building on this success, Franzese expanded his entrepreneurial portfolio in 2022 with the establishment of Franzese Wines, a brand specializing in wines.

Joseph "Joe" Amato

From his early twenties, Amato was drawn to the illicit world, finding himself entangled in its intricate web of power, influence, and danger. His ambition and shrewdness propelled him through the ranks of the Colombo crime family, eventually securing him the coveted position of capo, a role that demanded respect, loyalty, and an unwavering commitment to the organization's interests.

Amato's ascension to the upper echelons of the Colombo family was not without its challenges. The allure of illicit wealth and power often attracted the scrutiny of law enforcement, and Amato was not immune to their watchful eyes. In 2019, a web of legal troubles ensnared him, leading to his arrest and federal indictment for fraud and racketeering charges. The weight of these accusations, coupled with the potential consequences of conviction, presented a formidable obstacle to his continued dominance in the Mafia world.

Facing the daunting prospect of federal prosecution, Amato made a bold decision in 2021: he admitted guilt to the charges against him, a rare occurrence in the world of organized crime, demonstrated a willingness to face the repercussions of his choices and a departure from the traditional code of silence that often shrouded criminal activities.

The court's verdict reflected the severity of Amato's offenses, sentencing him to a substantial 70-month prison term. Currently, he serves his sentence in a federal prison located in Pennsylvania.

Vincent "Vinnie Unions" Ricciardo

A seasoned capo within the Colombo crime family, Vincent Ricciardo assumed control of the once-powerful Long Island crew previously led by the notorious John "Sonny" Franzese. This strategic move, orchestrated with the support of the family's leadership, aimed to revitalize the crew and reassert its dominance in the underworld of Long Island.

Ricciardo's ascension to the helm of the Franzese crew was not merely a matter of succession but a calculated decision based on his proven track record and reputation for brutality and unwavering loyalty. His rise through the ranks of the Colombo family had been marked by his ability to understand its dynamics and his willingness to adapt to its ever-changing landscape.

Under Ricciardo's leadership, the Long Island crew embarked on a period of renewed activity, seeking to reclaim its lost influence and assert its dominance in the region. However, their efforts were soon met with a formidable challenge in the form of law enforcement. On September 14, 2021, Ricciardo, along with several key members of the crew, was indicted on a series of criminal charges, including racketeering, extortion, and labor racketeering.

Dennis "Fat Dennis" DeLucia

A capo within the family, Dennis DeLucia held sway over the lucrative gambling operations in the Bronx. But his influence extended far beyond the backrooms of illicit gambling dens, as he was a respected figure within the family, known for his shrewdness and his unwavering loyalty to the Colombo organization.

In 2011, DeLucia's life took a dramatic turn when he found himself entangled in a major federal indictment that targeted the upper echelons of the family. Alongside acting boss Andrew Russo, soldiers Ilario Sessa and Joseph Savarese, and Angelo Spata, the son-in-law of Carmine Persico, DeLucia faced a series of serious criminal charges, including racketeering, extortion, and loan-sharking.

Facing the daunting prospect of a lengthy prison sentence, DeLucia made a strategic decision in 2012: he pleaded guilty to the extortion charges, acknowledging his involvement in the criminal scheme. In 2013, after serving a portion of his sentence, DeLucia was released from prison. His return to the streets of the Bronx marked a significant moment, as it remained unclear whether he would resume his former role in the Colombo family's gambling operations or if he would seek to distance himself from the Mafia ranks.

Salvatore "Sally Bread" Cambria

A figure shrouded in intrigue and notoriety, Salvatore Cambria held a prominent position within the Colombo crime family, ascending to the rank of capo and even serving as a street boss. His nickname, "Sally Bread," reflected his involvement in the family's extortion rackets, particularly targeting bakeries and restaurants, coercing them to purchase bread from his company at inflated prices.

In 2002, Cambria's involvement with the Colombo family came under public scrutiny during the trial of the Lucchese family's consigliere Joseph "Joe C." Caridi. Caridi, facing charges of racketeering and extortion, was accused of ordering a Freeport restaurant to purchase bread from Cambria's company, a blatant display of the family's influence and the extent of their extortion racket.

Cambria's prominence within the Colombo family continued to grow, and he eventually ascended to the position of capo. At the height of his power, Cambria even served as a street boss, a temporary leadership role that often accompanied periods of internal turmoil or power struggles within the family. This appointment underscored Cambria's trust and respect within the organization, as he was entrusted with the responsibility of maintaining order and overseeing the family's activities during a challenging time.

Luca DiMatteo

A seasoned capo within the family, Luca DiMatteo held a position of power and influence that extended beyond his official title as acting captain of the Lombardo crew. His younger brother, Ralph DiMatteo, served as the family's consigliere, further solidifying the brothers' prominence within the organization.

In 2015, he and his nephew, Luca "Lukey" DiMatteo, were indicted on a series of serious criminal charges, including racketeering conspiracy, loan-sharking, and operating an illegal gambling business in Brooklyn and elsewhere. DiMatteo pleaded guilty to the charges in 2016. At that time, he was sentenced to 33 months in prison. After serving a portion of his sentence, he was released in 2018.

Thomas "Tom Mix" Farese

Joseph Farese, a prominent figure within the family, held a position of power and influence that extended beyond his formal title as consigliere. His marriage to Suzanne, the daughter of Alphonse Persico, brother of the late Carmine Persico, solidified his connection to the Persico family, one of the most powerful factions within the Colombo organization.

In the 1970s, Farese relocated from Boston to Fort Lauderdale, Florida, where he established a strong foothold in the local underworld. His connection to Nicholas Forlano, a fellow Colombo mobster, further expanded his influence and provided him with access to lucrative criminal opportunities.

Farese's formal induction into the family in July 1978 marked a significant milestone in his criminal career. However, his ascent to prominence was not without its challenges. In 1980, he was convicted of marijuana smuggling, leading to a 30-year prison sentence. Despite this setback, Farese remained a respected figure within the family, his reputation for loyalty and resourcefulness intact.

Upon his release from prison in 1994, Farese faced another legal hurdle. In 1998, he pleaded guilty to money laundering charges, a reflection of his continued involvement in illicit activities. Despite these legal troubles, Farese managed to maintain his position of power within the Colombo family, demonstrating his resilience and adaptability.

In 2012, Farese faced new charges of loan-sharking and money laundering in south Florida. The charges stemmed from an investigation that relied heavily on recordings made by government informant Reynold Maragni. However, during Farese's September 2012 trial, the judge permitted his lawyer to inspect Maragni's wristwatch, which concealed a secret recording device. This revelation cast doubt on the reliability of Maragni's recordings and ultimately led to Farese's acquittal of all charges.

Despite his legal victories, Farese continued to face scrutiny from law enforcement. In April 2021, he faced federal healthcare fraud charges related to an orthotic brace supply company in Florida. Alongside partners, including Colombo associate Patrick Truglia, Farese was accused of engaging in kickback schemes to bribe medical providers and telehealth services for unnecessary brace prescriptions to elderly patients, charged to Medicare. Farese's case remained shrouded in secrecy, with court dockets sealed and the indictment refraining from explicitly referencing his connections to organized crime.

William "Billy" Russo

William "Billy" Russo, the youngest son of Andrew Russo, emerged as a prominent figure within the family, carrying on his father's legacy and etching his mark in the annals of organized crime.

Under the tutelage of his father and other seasoned members of the family, Russo diligently honed his skills, mastering the art of extortion, loan-sharking, and other illicit enterprises that formed the bedrock of the family's criminal activities. He proved to be a quick learner and a shrewd operator, capable of outmaneuvering rivals and securing lucrative opportunities for the family.

In 2007, his brother, Joseph "Jo Jo" Russo, passed away in prison, a loss that deeply affected him. Despite this personal tragedy, Russo remained committed to his role within the family, carrying on his father's legacy and continuing to exert his influence.

Joel Cacace

Born on April 9, 1941, Joel Cacace, also known as Joe Waverly, is an American mobster and former consigliere within the family. He faced a murder conviction in 2004 and remained in prison until his release in 2020.

Cacace grew up in a family deeply entrenched in organized crime: the Sheepshead Bay neighborhood in Brooklyn. His father, Joseph Cacace Sr., served as a capo in the Colombo family, and his uncle, Carmine Persico, led the family from 1973 to 1987.

Initiating his criminal career in the early 1960s, Cacace engaged in loan-sharking and enforcement activities under his father's guidance. Progressing swiftly, he ascended to the position of capo within the Colombo family by the early 1980s.

Following Persico's 1987 conviction for racketeering and a subsequent 139-year prison sentence, Cacace assumed the role of consigliere for the Colombo family, maintaining the position until 1997.

In 1997, Cacace faced arrest and murder charges related to the alleged ordering of Michael Meldish's killing, a former Colombo associate turned government witness. Found guilty of murder in 2004, Cacace received a 25-year-to-life prison sentence.

Released from incarceration in 2020 after serving 16 years, Cacace is presently under house arrest, supervised by federal authorities. Public opinion on Cacace is divisive, with some viewing him as a persistent threat deserving continued imprisonment, while others contend that he has undergone rehabilitation and should be permitted to resume a regular life.

Salvatore "Sally Boy" Castagno

Castagno is a significant figure in the underworld landscape of New York City, serving as a formidable capo and a key member of the family. Born into a family deeply entrenched in organized crime, Castagno's path toward a life of criminal activity was almost predetermined. His upbringing in the Gravesend-Coney Island neighborhood of Brooklyn exposed him to the inner workings of the family, providing him with a firsthand glimpse into the world of power, influence, and illicit gains.

Castagno's ascension within the Colombo family was closely intertwined with the dynamics of the "Gravesend-Coney Island crew," also known as the "East Third Street Clique." This faction, originally controlled by Benjamin "The Claw" Castellazzo, played a pivotal role in the family's operations, particularly in the areas of gambling, racketeering, and loan-sharking.

Under Castagno's leadership, the Gravesend-Coney Island crew gained notoriety for its ruthlessness and efficiency, becoming a feared entity in the underworld. Castagno, known for his strategic thinking and unwavering determination, proved adept at expanding the crew's influence and establishing lucrative criminal enterprises.

Sebastian and Gabriel Mills (The Twins)

Born on August 1, 1989, the catalyst for their entry into the criminal underworld occurred in 2000, when Al Franzese, a key figure in the family, journeyed to the Federal Correctional Complex in Butner, North Carolina. His mission was to visit the patriarch of the Colombo family, Carmine Persico, who was serving time behind bars.

During this visit, Persico, who sought to fulfill a murder task, approached Franzese with a request for the hit. Franzese found himself physically incapacitated due to an impending surgery, rendering him unable to carry out the task. It was at this critical juncture that the enigmatic twins, Sebastian and Gabriel Mills, caught Persico's attention.

Persico, ever the shrewd and strategic leader, seized the opportunity and approached the twins with a proposition: would they be willing to undertake the assigned hit in Franzese's stead? Without hesitation, the twins agreed to take on the perilous mission. This fateful decision would mark the beginning of their ascent as formidable hitmen within the family.

The successful execution of the hit not only solidified the twins' standing within the Colombo family but also earned them a fearsome reputation as ruthless and efficient enforcers. From that moment forward, Sebastian and Gabriel Mills became synonymous with the term "top hitmen," known for their willingness to accept any contract, regardless of the target's prominence or the complexity of the assignment.

Giovanni Cerbone

Cerbone joined the crew of Joseph Amato, a powerful figure within the organization. Cerbone's involvement in the illegal activities drew the attention of law enforcement, leading to his arrest on drug and money laundering charges.

The weight of the evidence against Cerbone was undeniable. He had been deeply involved in the distribution of cocaine, marijuana, and oxycodone pills, reaping substantial profits from his illicit enterprises. Moreover, he had devised elaborate schemes to launder the proceeds of his crimes, seeking to conceal the origins of his ill-gotten wealth. Faced with the overwhelming evidence against him, Cerbone opted to plead guilty to the charges, acknowledging his involvement in the family's criminal activities. On November 5, 2015, he was sentenced to 70 months in prison and was released in 2021.

Michael Uvino

Born in New York City in the year 1965, Uvino found himself inexorably drawn into the Mafia from a tender age. It was during the crucial formative years of his life that his entanglement with the family commenced, setting the stage for a journey through the Mafia.

Uvino's career was marked by his active participation in a myriad of racketeering schemes. One of the most significant chapters in his criminal saga unfolded through his pivotal role in orchestrating an exploit that targeted a high-ranking official within a construction union based in the borough of Queens. Uvino, along with his colleagues, forced the union official into a paying monthly sum of $2,600. This financial demand symbolized the effective placement of the union official under the control of the Colombo family.

The year 2001 proved to be a critical moment in the life of Uvino, as his involvement in the extortion scheme finally attracted the vigilant gaze of law enforcement. Uvino faced the weight of the evidence against him. In the end, he was convicted of a 41-month prison term.

CHAPTER 7
POPULAR CULTURE AND THE COLOMBO CRIME FAMILY

Throughout its existence, the Colombo family has seamlessly woven itself into the fabric of popular culture. The family's multifaceted image has been meticulously crafted through a diverse range of portrayals across various media forms, leaving an enduring impact on public perception. Whether depicted as the idealized figures reminiscent of *The Godfather* or through the gritty realism portrayed in *Goodfellas*, these cinematic and literary representations have played a pivotal role in shaping the collective consciousness regarding the family. Beyond mere entertainment, these depictions have transcended into cultural artifacts that influence how the community as a whole views the organization, and also the family's self-perception. The intertwining of real-life events with fictionalized narratives has added layers of complexity to the Colombo family's cultural legacy, further solidifying its place in the broader tapestry of organized crime's portrayal in popular media.

The earliest representations of the family in popular culture often painted a romanticized picture of the gangster lifestyle. Films like *The Godfather*, released in 1972, portrayed the Mafia world as one of power, wealth, and glamour, downplaying the inherent violence and brutality that lay beneath the surface. These depictions, while captivating audiences, contributed to a distorted perception of organized crime, romanticizing the lifestyle of a group known for its ruthless and corrupt practices.

As time progressed, the portrayal of the family in popular culture evolved, shifting towards a more realistic and nuanced representation. Films like *Goodfellas*, released in 1990, delved into the darker aspects of the Mafia, exposing the prevalent violence, corruption, and betrayals that pervaded the organization. While these portrayals helped dispel some myths and misconceptions about the family, they also reinforced an image of the organization as menacing, intimidating, and morally reprehensible.

The indelible presence of the Colombo crime family in popular culture extends far beyond the silver screen, permeating various facets of artistic expression such as literature, music, and a myriad of other media forms. Within the realm of literature, notable works like Nicholas Pileggi's *Wiseguy*, which served as the basis for the iconic film *Goodfellas*, delve into the intricate nuances of the Mafia's inner workings. This kind of novel provides readers with a captivating and detailed exploration of the complex dynamics, motivations, and relationships that drive the members of organized crime families.

In addition to literature, the influence of the Colombo family resonates in the melodies and lyrics of music. Iconic songs like Billy Joel's "New York State of Mind" and Frank Sinatra's "My Way" have contributed to perpetuating the romanticized image of the gangster in popular culture. These musical compositions, with their evocative themes and narratives, capture the essence of a bygone era and encapsulate the allure of the Mafia lifestyle. Through the emotive power of music, the image of the gangster is further immortalized, appealing to audiences and perpetuating the mystique associated with organized crime.

Moreover, the portrayal of Colombo family members has found its way into television series, documentaries, and even visual art, creating a multifaceted narrative that explores the various dimensions of organized crime. This cross-disciplinary representation underscores the enduring fascination with the Mafia, captivating audiences and providing a rich tapestry of narratives that contribute to the family's cultural legacy.

These diverse portrayals of the family in popular culture have collectively contributed to the public's understanding of the organization, shaping perceptions of its power, influence, and inherent criminality. They have also played a role in shaping the family's self-image, influencing how its members view themselves and their place in the world of organized crime.

While the idealized portrayals of the early days have largely given way to more realistic and gritty representations, the allure of the family's legacy continues to resonate in popular culture. The organization's history, fraught with violence, power struggles, and tales of both loyalty and betrayal, remains a source of fascination, providing fodder for stories that explore the depths of human nature and the dark underbelly of society.

Impact of These Portrayals on Public Perception of Colombo Crime Family

Portrayals that Glamorize the Mafia Lifestyle

The romanticized portrayal of the family, as seen in films like *The Godfather* and *Goodfellas*, has had a profound impact on public perception, shaping a narrative that is far removed from the harsh realities of organized crime. These cinematic depictions have presented the family as a powerful and opulent organization, rife with glamour and intrigue, inadvertently glorifying a lifestyle built on violence, corruption, and exploitation.

The Godfather, released in 1972, stands as a prime example of this romanticized portrayal. The film's success and enduring popularity have cemented the image of the Mafia as a world of power, wealth, and family loyalty, overlooking the inherent criminality and moral failings that underlie this lifestyle. The film's characters, particularly Vito Corleone, are portrayed as complex and charismatic figures, evoking a sense of admiration and fascination among viewers.

Similarly, *Goodfellas*, released in 1990, while delving deeper into the darker aspects of the Mafia, still retains a degree of romanticization. The film's fast-paced narrative, coupled with its depiction of the camaraderie and excitement of the gangster lifestyle, has contributed to a distorted perception of organized crime. While the film exposes the violence and corruption that pervades the Mafia, it also paints a glamorous picture of luxury, showcasing the material wealth, social standing, and perceived sense of power that the Mafia lifestyle promises.

These movies have had a significant impact on public perception of the family. They have perpetuated the belief that the Mafia is a glamorous and powerful organization, inhabited by figures who wield extraordinary influence and operate outside the constraints of law and morality. This distorted perception has far-reaching consequences, not only in shaping public understanding of organized crime but also in influencing the self-perception of the family itself.

The romanticized portrayal has also contributed to the mythologization of the Mafia, elevating its members to the status of almost legendary figures. This mythologization has obscured the true nature of organized crime, downplaying the violence, corruption, and human costs associated with its activities.

In reality, the family is far removed from the glamorous image portrayed in films. The organization is riddled with internal conflicts, power struggles, and betrayals, and its members are constantly under the scrutiny of law enforcement. The lifestyle of a Mafia figure is not one of luxury and glamour; it is a life of violence, fear, and uncertainty, constantly teetering on the brink of destruction.

Depiction of Violence and Corruption

In contrast to the romanticized portrayals that have often dominated popular culture, other depictions of the Colombo family, such as the HBO television series *The Sopranos* and the non-fiction novel *Wiseguy* by Nicholas Pileggi, have offered a more grounded and unflinching look at the dark realities of organized crime. These works have eschewed the glamour and allure that often characterize portrayals of the Mafia, instead delving into the gritty underbelly of the organization, exposing the violence, corruption, and moral compromises that lie at its core.

The Sopranos, which aired from 1999 to 2007, took inspiration from New Jersey's often-overlooked DeCavalcante Mafia crime family, and revolutionized the depiction of the Mafia, showcasing the complexities and contradictions of its members. The show's protagonist, Tony Soprano, is not a larger-than-life figure shrouded in mystery and intrigue; he is a flawed and relatable individual, grappling with the pressures of family, work, and his moral compass. *The Sopranos* explored the psychological toll of a life steeped in violence and betrayal, challenging the romanticized notion of the Mafia as a world of power and glamour.

These more realistic depictions have served as a powerful lens, pulling back the curtain on the darker facets of the Mafia's existence. Through narratives that delve into the intricacies of organized crime, works in various media forms have effectively exposed the inherent violence, corruption, and moral decay that permeate the Mafia's operations. By peeling away the layers of mystique and glamour that had previously shrouded the criminal underworld, these portrayals have brought forth a stark and unfiltered representation, showcasing the harsh realities that define the family's existence. These works have accomplished more than just entertaining; they have become vehicles for social commentary and heightened public awareness.

CONCLUSION

By this, a comprehensive explanation of the history of the Colombo family from its founding until the present day was completed, mentioning the most important historical events that occurred, including conflicts and alliances, and the most important figures and names that had the greatest impact on shaping the history of the Mafia in the twentieth century, from Leaders, commanders, and rebels. It can be said that this book covers the most important information that the readers might be looking for and answers the questions in their minds about that period, which was filled with many important events.

The historical trajectory of the Colombo crime family unfolds through a series of distinct stages, each leaving an indelible mark on the organization's legacy. Our manuscript delves into the intricate narrative of this family, tracing its evolution from the foundational era initiated by Joe Profaci to the leadership of Joseph Colombo. It also covers the subsequent stage characterized as a period of prosperity under the helm of Carmen Persico, and the stage marked by decline and internal as well as external conflicts.

The Mafia is a very secretive and closed organization, meaning that no one has the right to join it, regardless of who he is, unless he meets the necessary conditions for that. There is certain training that every new member must go through before actually becoming an official member. He must swear an oath of loyalty to the organization. In addition, he must threaten or kill someone for them to accept his entry into it. Meaning that they would be able to hold something dangerous against him to threaten him with it in case he thinks about leaving the Mafia or turning against it. This situation makes obtaining accurate details about the insides of the family not easy. Therefore, a large portion of the information and sources have been traced back to investigations by law enforcement authorities and the testimonies of defectors from the family and those previously close to it.

However, through this manuscript, we provided a comprehensive historical overview of the family, its secrets, symbols, operations, criminal activities, and alliances. After reviewing the family's history, we must ask the basic question that will determine its future and the nature of its relationships with other families and with society: Is the Mafia an ongoing reality that must be dealt with as a fait accompli? Or are there laws that will succeed in curbing organized crime?

REFERENCES

Colombo Crime Family LEADERSHIP TIMELINE. (n.d). NCS. https://www.nationalcrimesyndicate.com/colombo-crime-family-leadership-timeline/

Colombo Crime Family. (n.d). Academic Accelerator. https://academic-accelerator.com/encyclopedia/colombo-crime-family

The Colombo Crime Family. (2023, Jan 31). Gangstersinc. https://gangstersinc.org/profiles/blogs/the-colombo-crime-family

The Colombo Family. (n.d). The New York Mafia. https://thenewyorkmafia.com/colombo-family/

Gage, N. (1972, Apr 08). *Grudges Against Gallo Date to 'War' With Profaci.* NyTimes. https://www.nytimes.com/1972/04/08/archives/grudges-against-gallo-date-to-war-with-profaci.html

Guy, T. (n.d). *Joe Profaci – The Olive Oil King.* The New York Mafia. https://thenewyorkmafia.com/guiseppe-joe-profaci/

Guy, T. (n.d). *The Profaci-Gallo War of 1961-1963.* The New York Mafia. https://thenewyorkmafia.com/gallo-profaci-war/

Hunt, T. (n.d). *King of the Brooklyn docks: Albert Anastasia.* The American Mafia. https://mafiahistory.us/a009/f_albertanastasia.html

Jackman, T. (2019, Mar 15). *New York Mafia still active, but flashy 'mob hits' decline as witnesses flip and law hits harder.* Washington Post. https://www.washingtonpost.com/crime-law/2019/03/15/new-york-mafia-still-active-flashy-mob-hits-decline-witnesses-flip-law-hits-harder/

Joe Gallo Biography. (n.d). The Famous People. https://www.thefamouspeople.com/profiles/joe-gallo-11698.php

Joe Profaci Biography. (n.d). The Famous People. https://www.thefamouspeople.com/profiles/joe-profaci-24586.php

Joseph Gallo. (1998, Jul 20). Encyclopedia Britannica. https://www.britannica.com/biography/Joseph-Gallo

Joseph Profaci. (2007, Oct 25). Encyclopedia Britannica. https://www.britannica.com/biography/Joseph-Profaci

Mafia in the United States. (2019, Jun 19). History. https://www.history.com/topics/crime/mafia-in-the-united-states

Merrill, B. (2014, Jan 23). *Carmine Persico.* Prezi. https://prezi.com/tnivnv1dfeud/carmine-persico/

Metych, M. (2022, Oct 04). *Colombo crime family.* Encyclopedia Britannica. https://www.britannica.com/topic/Colombo-crime-family

Redd, W. (2022, Feb 11). *How Joe Gallo Started A Mafia War — And Paid For It With His Life.* ATI. https://allthatsinteresting.com/crazy-joe-gallo

Retter, E. (2019, Mar 10). *How Mafia boss The Snake who once 'caught a bullet with his teeth' rose to power.* Mirror. https://www.mirror.co.uk/news/us-news/how-mafia-boss-snake-who-14115615

Reyes, R. (2022. Feb 05). *Colombo crime family boss is freed on $5 million bond.* Daily Mail. https://www.dailymail.co.uk/news/article-10479845/Colombo-crime-family-leader-Ralph-DiMatteo-freed-Friday-Brooklyn-jail-5-million-bond.html

Robbins, T. (2022, July 23). *In the Mafia's Shadow, a Son Honors His Father.* NewYorker. https://www.newyorker.com/culture/persons-of-interest/in-the-mafias-shadow-a-son-honors-his-father

Seaver, C. (n.d). *The Bloody Rise and Fall of "Crazy Joe" Gallo.* History Defined. https://www.historydefined.net/joe-gallo/

Serena, K. (2018, Dec 28). *Carmine Persico Spent 46 Years As A Mafia Boss, 32 Of Them Behind Bars.* ATI. https://allthatsinteresting.com/carmine-persico

Shirey, P. (2022, Sep 08). *The Offer: Joe Gallo And Mobster Link To The Godfather Explained.* Screen Rant. https://screenrant.com/offer-show-joe-gallo-mob-godfather-connection-explained/

The social networks of Joseph Profaci. (n.d). Mafiagenealogy. https://mafiagenealogy.com/2023/02/01/the-social-networks-of-joseph-profaci/

U.S. Attorney's Office. (2009, Dec 19). *Colombo Family "Street Boss" Indicted as Head of Massachusetts RICO Crew.* THE FBI.

https://archives.fbi.gov/archives/boston/press-releases/2009/bs121709.htm

Walsh, S. (2000, June 15). *120 Charged in Probe Of Mob on Wall St.* The Washington Post. https://www.washingtonpost.com/archive/politics/2000/06/15/120-charged-in-probe-of-mob-on-wall-st/50ee710e-6e13-4c3e-8b0e-7a47f317bf12/

Printed in Great Britain
by Amazon